Judaism through Children's Books

A Resource for Teachers and Parents

Ellen Musikant
and Sue Grass

A.R.E. Publishing, Inc.
Denver, Colorado

Book cover on page 60: THE CHRISTMAS MENORAHS: HOW A TOWN FOUGHT HATE by Janice Cohn, illustrated by Bill Farnsworth. Copyright © 1995 Albert Whitman & Company. Cover reprinted with permission.

Book cover on page 90: "Cover Art" copyright © 1999 by Dan Andreasen, illustrations, from STREETS OF GOLD by Rosemary Wells, illustrated by Dan Andreasen. Used by permission of Dial Books for Young Readers, an imprint of Penguin Putnam Books for Young Readers, a division of Penguin Putnam Inc.

Book cover on page 124: From PENNY AND THE FOUR QUESTIONS by Nancy Krulik, illustrated by Marian Young. Illustration copyright © 1993 by Marian Young. Reprinted by permission of Scholastic Inc.

Book cover on page 159: "Cover illustration" by Elizabeth Sayles, copyright © 1994 by Elizabeth Sayles, from THE NIGHT CROSSING by Karen Ackerman, illustrated by Elizabeth Sayles. Used by permission of Random House Children's Books, a division of Random House, Inc.

Published by:
A.R.E. Publishing, Inc.
Denver, Colorado

Library of Congress Card Number 2001086119
ISBN 0-86705-050-0

© A.R.E. Publishing, Inc. 2001

Printed in the United States of America
10   9   8   7   6   5   4   3   2   1

All rights reserved. No part of this book may be reproduced in any form or by any means without permission in writing from the publisher.

Only learning that is enjoyed will be learned well.
(Judah ha-Nasi)

When a day passes, it is no longer there. What remains of it? Nothing more than a story. If stories weren't told or books weren't written, man would live like the beasts, only for the day . . . The whole world, all human life, is one long story.
("Naftali the Storyteller & His Horse, Sus" in *Stories for Children* by I.B. Singer)

Acknowledgments

We would like to thank the following people for their contributions to this project: Martha Cohen, for her help in book selection and for making Jewish books special; Jacob Gross, for finding *A Time of Angels*; Rachel Charlotte Hodes, for reading many of the books and for being a wonderful daughter; Fran Lee, the quintessential librarian, for her many suggestions and research assistance; Lisa Messeri, for dreaming up activities for the PK set; Peter Messeri, for supporting this undertaking; Toby Staenberg, for being a good friend and inspired preschool teacher who listened patiently; Anita Wenner for additional research; Adam Yourtz, for being a great model for the cover photo; and Audrey Friedman Marcus and Rabbi Raymond A. Zwerin of A.R.E. Publishing, Inc., for their encouragement and skillful editing.

CONTENTS

	Introduction	ix
1	Bible: In the Beginning	1
2	Ethics: Doing the Right Thing	31
3	Folklore: From Generation To Generation	61
4	History: 4,000 Years and Counting	91
5	Holidays: Let's Celebrate!	125
6	Holocaust: Remembering to Remember	157
7	Life Cycle: To Everything There Is a Season	191

INTRODUCTION

Background

Recently, Ellen Musikant, one of the authors of this volume, was a visiting artist at Temple B'nai Or in Morristown, New Jersey. She was conducting a workshop with the fifth grade students, and began by asking what stories we as Jews tell. Hands shot up all over the room. One girl pointed out that we read the story of Queen Esther at Purim. A boy said that we read the story of the Exodus and the Ten Plagues at Passover. Still another said we tell the story of creation at the New Year. Jewish holidays and festivals are certainly replete with stories. So are our holy books. The Torah, the Prophets, the Writings, the Talmud, among others, are so full of stories that stories have been written about those stories. These are the *midrashim*.

The Jewish people are also brimming over with tales to tell. Our history is long and rich and filled with drama. A treasure trove of folklore and literary works explains and defines the varied experiences. It is no wonder that there are countless books categorized as Judaica. And this is no less true for the juvenile bookshelf.

In recent years, there has been an explosion in the number of books published for children. We imagine this is due in large part to a healthy economy and an affluent, well educated generation of parents and grandparents. Buying books for one's child or for one's school is no longer a matter of buying what is available (which used to be so limited), but of purchasing those books that can add significantly to a child's Jewish education. *Judaism through Children's Books* will help maximize the quality of the books you use, read, and enjoy with your students (and/or with your own children).

About This Book

Jewish literature addresses Jewish topics. It can be read by anyone, but its focus is on the Jewish experience. For this book, we chose seven specific areas to explore that we felt would most likely be part of a standard Religious School or Day School curriculum. These make up the seven chapters of this book.

In selecting books for inclusion in this volume, we considered their read-aloud qualities for younger children and intellectual accessibility for older children. We looked for compelling stories, beautiful language, and an overarching respect for Judaism.

The chapters are arranged alphabetically by topic. The books in each chapter are arranged alphabetically within each recommended age group. Chapter 1, "Bible: In the Beginning," features books that relate stories from scripture and books that introduce concepts of God. Chapter 2, "Ethics: Doing the Right Thing," concerns itself with books that pose questions of morality and that provide models for leading an ethical life. Chapter 3, "Folklore: From Generation To Generation," presents some of the best folk literature available for children today. Many of these books can be used in conjunction with other topics, such as holidays and ethics. Chapter 4, "History: 4,000 Years and Counting," spans the Jewish experience from biblical times to life as an American immigrant. Chapter 5, "Holidays: Let's Celebrate!" highlights books about Shabbat and other holidays and festivals. Chapter 6, "Holocaust: Remembering to Remember," attempts to explore this dark period through the different experiences of those who survived and those who didn't, and from those who hid, those who were sent to the camps, and those who managed to escape. And, finally, Chapter 7, "Life Cycle: To Everything There Is a Season," covers the major events in Jewish life. Some of the books in this last section are on topics particular to Jews, such as becoming a Bar or Bat Mitzvah, and others are on universal subjects, such as aging and dying.

Using This Book

This book has been written for anyone who works with Jewish youth — Religious School teachers, Day School teachers, librarians, youth group leaders, and parents. It is designed to save you time and to steer you toward some of the best books available at this writing.

Each chapter begins with a brief introduction to the topic, followed by a list of featured books. Each description of a featured book begins with its title, author, illustrator, publisher, copyright date, number of pages, and a recommended age group. It also indicates whether the book is best read alone, read aloud, or read together. A brief summary of the book is followed by a list of Main Ideas, Discussion Starters, and Activities to enhance and extend the experience of the book. The activities were collected from studying written curricular materials, talking with Jewish teachers, and adapting projects we have used successfully in various settings. Remember, though, these suggestions are meant solely as departure points. Bring your own creativity to bear when deciding on activities. The last section of each chapter is called "For Further Reading" and consists of an annotated list of recommended books on the topic. These are arranged alphabetically by age group. In some instances, a book is cross-referenced with another chapter.

Teacher Preparation

For all those who will be using these books, whether in class, in the library, or at home, we recommend that you first read each book yourself and see if you agree that it is worthwhile and appropriate for your children or for the children you teach. Try out projects ahead of time so you can streamline your preparation. Generally, these books stand on their own and you do not need to introduce them with additional information. But many of the books may raise lots of questions among the children, so be prepared.

Depending on the age group with which you are working, it may be more effective to do one or more of the listed activities after reading the book, but before a discussion. Very often, the experience of doing a project will heighten curiosity and deepen understanding.

When deciding which books to incorporate into your lessons, consider how each fits with your existing curriculum. A book such as *Ten Good Rules*, which is featured for PK in Chapter 2, "Ethics: Doing the Right Thing," would work equally well when you are teaching Shavuot in the spring. Perhaps your curriculum does not have a folktale sequence, but given the wealth of available resources presented in Chapter 3, "Folklore: From Generation To Generation," you could design such a sequence and through it teach other areas of Jewish concern, such as holidays, history, and ethics.

Conclusion

In writing this book, it was necessary to make many difficult choices. We realized that we could include just a small number of the many noteworthy books for Jewish children that are available. And to make our task even more difficult, wonderful new books for this audience seemingly appear every day. So we learned the wisdom of the passage from *Pirke Avot* 2:21: "It is not your duty to complete the task, but you are not free to desist from it."

This book was written for you — the front line educator, whether you be teacher or parent — to enable you to enrich your teaching through Jewish literature. We hope that the work we have done for you will make your teaching experience a little easier, as well as help your students and your children to become more interested in Jewish subject matter.

Key to Activity Icons

 Main Ideas

Discussion Starters

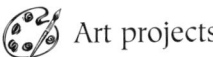 Art projects

♪ Music projects

👁 Looking at things, Field trip

🌳 Nature/ecology, planting

📖 Read aloud, Tell a story, Sequence a story

Creative writing

? Riddle

Cooking, Tasting

🎭 Drama

Rank order a list, Make a list

📚 Research

 Family tree

 Map work

 Tzedakah, Action project

 Brainstorm

 Discussion, Interview, Debate

 Time capsule

 Guest speaker

 Watch a video

 Show & tell

 Arrange a workshop

 Teach a skill

 Compare & contrast

 Say prayers/blessings

 Games

Chapter 1

Bible:
In the Beginning

When Ellen turned 40, she decided it was time to read the Torah. Though it is now a decade later, she remembers the sunny winter afternoon when she picked up her JPS translation, stretched out on the sofa, and began to read. She read several chapters, all but holding her breath, and then let out a sigh. She put down the book for a moment, turned to her husband, and said, "This really is a good book!" Well, she's been reading and studying the text ever since, keeping in mind *Pirke Avot* 5:26: "Turn it [the Torah] and turn it again, for everything is in it, and contemplate it, and grow gray and old over it, and stir not from it, for you can have no better rule than this."

Featured Books

Light: The First Seven Days (PK)
Why Noah Chose the Dove (PK)
In Our Image (K-3)
Jonah and the Two Great Fish (K-3)
Old Turtle (K-3)
Joseph (2-4)
King Solomon and the Queen of Sheba (2-4)
The Book of Tens (4-6)
King Solomon and His Magic Ring (4-6)
But God Remembered (6-8)
Miriam (6-8)
Escape from Egypt (9-12)

Note: The word "Midrash" is used frequently in this chapter. It can be translated as "search and explain." The Midrash refers to the body of literature which includes parables, sayings, and stories that provide explanations or expositions of Bible text. A Midrash refers to a particular story or teaching. Midrashim is the plural.

Light: The First Seven Days

By Sarah Waldman
Illustrated by Neil Waldman
Harcourt Brace, 1993
32 pages
ISBN 0-15-220870-4
PK

This is a simple retelling of the Genesis story of creation written by the illustrator's 13-year-old daughter. She follows the text closely, but adds some beautiful verbal punctuation and an appeal for people to protect the Earth. Neil Waldman's illustrations are vibrant.

Main Ideas

- The world was created by God in six days and on the seventh day God rested.
- God's creation is good.
- People must protect creation.

Discussion Starters

- What is the best part about Creation?
- What can people do to protect the Earth?
- If you were going to create an animal, what would it look like?

Activities

 Neil Waldman's illustrations remind us of stained glass. Hold up the book so the children can see a picture. Then hold up different crayons and have the children decide whether that color is in the picture. Do not lead them toward black, grey, or white. Give each child a sheet of white or manila construction paper. Lay out the selected crayons before them, and have them draw a part of creation. Suggest a flower, an animal, a tree, etc. Next, have the children use black tempera paint and chubby brushes and have them paint over the entire sheet. The paint should bead up over the crayon, but adhere to the places on the paper where there is no crayon. Let the pictures dry. You can mount these "Stained Glass" pictures onto larger sheets of black paper.

Create a "soundscape" with the children. First, read the book so the children can see the pictures. Then, ask them to close their eyes and read it to them again, very quietly. Next, tell them to imagine what things sounded like way back "in the beginning." As you read the book again, have them create the sounds with their voices and with their bodies — clapping, snapping, etc.

Go outside with the children to notice and enjoy creation. Play a game of *I Spy*. Example: You say, "I see something that is brown, fell from a tree, and has lots of tiny shelves." The kids answer: "A pine cone!" Teach the blessing said when noticing a beautiful sight in nature:

בָּרוּךְ אַתָּה יְיָ אֱלֹהֵינוּ מֶלֶךְ הָעוֹלָם עֹשֶׂה מַעֲשֵׂה בְרֵאשִׁית.

Baruch Atah Adonai Elohaynu Melech HaOlam Oseh Ma'aseh V'Reysheet.

Blessed is the Eternal our God, Ruler of the Universe, Who creates and recreates the world anew.

Why Noah Chose the Dove

By Isaac Bashevis Singer,
Translated by Elizabeth Shub
Illustrated by Eric Carle
Farrar, Straus and Giroux, 1987
32 pages
ISBN 0-374-43820-7
PK

Master storyteller I.B. Singer has added a twist to the Genesis story of Noah by enlivening the boastful personalities of all the animals — all, that is, except the dove, whose modesty is well rewarded. Eric Carle's illustrations are the recognizable cut-out collages made famous in his well-known book *The Very Hungry Caterpillar.*

Main Ideas

- God sent a flood to punish people because they had sinned.
- God told Noah to build an ark and save himself, his family, and all the animals.
- You don't have to boast to be recognized.

Discussion Starters

- The dove says: "Each one of us has something the other doesn't have, given us by God who created us all." What do you think is special about you?
- If you could be one of the animals in this book, which one would you be? Why?
- Has anyone ever said anything to "belittle" you, make you feel like you weren't as good as you thought you were? How did that make you feel? What did you do about your feelings?

Activities

 Create animals. Cut out of oaktag enough heads, bodies, legs, wings, and tails for each member of the class. Pre-punch holes at the "joints." Take brown paper grocery bags and put all the heads in one, bodies in another, and so forth. Have the children reach into each bag to get all the body parts they will need to create their own very special animals. Then, assemble the animals using metal fasteners. Explain how Adam named all the animals (Genesis 2:19 and 20), then ask them to name theirs.

 Sing the following to the tune of "The Farmer in the Dell":

Noah's in the ark, Noah's in the ark, Hi-ho the water rose, Noah's in the ark.

Noah picks a wife . . . The wife picks a child . . . The child picks a lion . . . Elephant . . . Monkey . . . Bear . . . Squirrel . . . Cat . . . Leopard . . . Dog . . . Sheep . . . Bee . . . Horse . . . Giraffe . . . Hippo . . . Crocodile . . . Parrot . . . Rooster . . . Dove

The dove flies alone, the dove flies alone . . . Hi-ho the water rose, the dove flies alone.

 Make a dove using mixed media. Draw an outline of a dove for each child on a piece of cardboard. Have glue, white feathers and white tissue paper, yellow construction paper triangles (the beak), and googly eyes available. Demonstrate each step in making a dove, then have the children make their doves step by step. Add feathers and tissue paper, then add eyes and beak. Finally, give each child a very lightweight stick with leaves on it to glue to the dove's beak.

In Our Image: God's First Creatures

By Nancy Sohn Swartz
Illustrated by Melanie Hall
Jewish Lights Publishing, 1998
32 pages
ISBN 1-0879045-99-0
K-3

"Let Us make humans in Our image, after Our likeness." The question posed and answered in this picture book is: who is "Us" and what is "Our likeness"? The author proposes that "Us" is all that had been created so far, the animals, moon, stars, and waters. A crisis occurs when God says that the people will "have dominion over . . . every living thing . . ." The animals are frightened and take flight, but are reassured when God describes the people as partners in creation. This is a beautifully illustrated introduction to a discussion of the nature of humankind.

Main Ideas

- God is the Creator.
- People were created last and with varied characteristics.
- People are responsible for caring for the world and all creation.

Discussion Starters

- If you were helping God create people, what suggestions would you make?
- What do you think is the most important thing about you?
- What can people do to take care of the world and its animals?

Activities

 In this version of the creation story, all the animals want to create people with attributes like their own. The fish want them to swim, the bee wants them to be lazy, etc. It is interesting to think about how other people perceive us. Do they see us as we are, or how they want us to be? For this project, give a child-sized piece of craft paper to each child. Have a child lie down on it and have a partner trace an outline. Then, have each child decorate with wallpaper samples, yarn, and markers his or her partner's image. A discussion could follow about each artists' choices.

 Take a trip to a zoo or farm or animal shelter and watch the behavior of the different animals. Have each child pick one and "introduce" it as though the animal was going to be a guest on a talk show.

 As a class, raise money and donate it to organizations such as the following. The money could be raised by having a seeds/bulbs/plant sale.

The Nature Conservancy
4245 N. Fairfax Dr., Suite 100
Arlington, VA 22203
800-628-6860
www.tnc.org

Save the Whales
P.O. Box 2397
Venice, CA 90291
800-WHALE-65
www.savethewhales.org

Sierra Club
85 Second St., 2nd floor
San Francisco, CA 94105
415-977-5500
www.sierraclub.com

Jonah and the Two Great Fish

Written and illustrated by Mordicai Gerstein
Simon & Schuster Books for Young Readers, 1997
ISBN 0-689-81373-2
32 pages
K-3

READ ALOUD

The author draws on the rich *midrashic* tradition surrounding the story of Jonah to create a unique and sometimes humorous version of the tale. Due to his insecurities, the reluctant prophet Jonah runs away from his responsibilities and from God. He is found and finally agrees to go to Ninevah and warn the people there of impending divine destruction. When they repent and God shows mercy, Jonah takes issue with the results. But he learns that saving lives is far more important than saving his pride.

Main Ideas

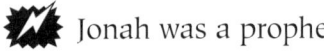 Jonah was a prophet.

 Even prophets can feel insecure.

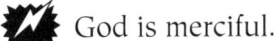 God is merciful.

Discussion Starters

- What do you think is meant by this line: "Jonah is too comfortable," thought God. "He will never change his mind and do as I asked."

- Has there ever been a time when you have been asked to do a job you felt you wouldn't be able to do? Did you try to do it? What happened?

- What would life be like if there was no chance to ask forgiveness or to be forgiven? What is the difference in how you feel when you say "I'm sorry" and when you say "That's all right, I forgive you"?

Activities

 Read again what the author says it was like inside the first fish. Ask the children to imagine the most perfect place to live. Place a large pad of newsprint on an easel. Have the children dictate their ideas of a place that is so comfortable they wouldn't want to leave. Older children can write a composition entitled: "Comfy, Cozy, and All for Me."

 Plant a seed. Give each child a plastic cup and a spoon. Have potting soil in a bucket for them to scoop into their cups. Give each child a seed. Nasturtium seeds are easy to handle, grow quickly, and have big broad leaves. Keep the seeds in the correct environment (read seed package), and post a chart in the classroom to measure how long it takes the seed to sprout and grow. Once the seeds begin to grow, return to the part in the story when the vine grows overnight and then withers. Discuss what a miracle is.

 Study the illustrations and how God is depicted, using negative space and the stars, moon, and birds. Give the children paper doilies or stencils and tape them to a piece of black paper. Give them white Cray-pas, chalk, or pastels to color *gently* over the doilies. Remove them and see the negative images that are created.

Old Turtle

By Douglas Wood
Illustrated by Cheng-Khee Chee
Pfeifer-Hamilton Publishers, 1992
48 pages
ISBN 0-938586-48-3
K-3

READ ALOUD

This is a lovely fable-like tale about the argument among the animals as to the true nature of God, as well as the lack of respect for the world by human beings when they move away from God. Told beautifully and simply, this story is an excellent supplement to any lesson on Genesis or God, and is a must-have for any synagogue library.

Main Ideas

- What is God?
- Everyone's perspective is valid.
- Coming together in understanding can be for the good of all.

Discussion Starters

- What do you think God is? Where is God? Why is God?
- Do you think Old Turtle is right? If not, is anyone else in the book right? Who?
- Which is your favorite picture, and why?

Activities

 Help children make a list of things they could do to show respect for the world and for God. As a group, pick one of the things on the list and do it. (For example, "Clean up the world." To do this, take a walk and collect the trash along the way.)

 Make a big poster with "God is . . . " in the center and, using all different colors, brainstorm with students and write down what they say.

 Have everyone write a poem of what God means to them.

Joseph

Retold and illustrated by Brian Wildsmith
Eerdmans Books for Young Readers, 1997
32 pages
ISBN 0-8028-5161-4
Grades 2-4

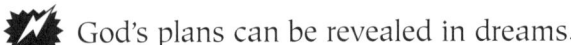

The Joseph story begins when he receives the coat of many colors from his father Jacob. It continues to the time when his family is reunited in Egypt. This book features glorious illustrations that colorfully describe the life of tribesmen in the wilderness and the architectural splendor of ancient Egypt.

Main Ideas

- The Bible tells the story of Joseph.
- God's plans can be revealed in dreams.
- Jealousy can lead to tragedy.

Discussion Starters

- Do you think it was wise of Jacob to give Joseph the coat of many colors?
- Jealousy rears its ugly head twice in this story. Joseph's brothers, and also Potiphar, are jealous of Joseph and they severely punish him. Have you ever felt jealous of someone? What happened?
- Why didn't Joseph immediately reveal himself to his brothers?

Activities

 Listen to a tape or CD of *Joseph and the Amazing Technicolor Dreamcoat*. Better yet, attend a production of this fun Andrew Lloyd Webber adaptation of the Joseph story. Discuss why the composer chose particular types of music to express each section of the tale.

 The technicolor dreamcoat in Lloyd Webber's musical is a reference to Joseph's "coat of many colors." The Hebrew is כְּתֹנֶת פַּסִּים (*k'toe-net pah-seem*) and is sometimes translated as "ornamental tunic." Today the word "*pah-seem*" might be translated as "striped." Supply children with a cutout of a tunic/coat and collage materials, such as wallpapers, yarns and trims. Have them use these materials to interpret the Hebrew phrase.

 Each part of this story is necessary in order for Jacob's family to go from Canaan down to Goshen where the Israelites lived for centuries until "a new king arose in Egypt who did not know Joseph" (Exodus 1:8). This sets the stage for the greatest story of the Jewish people, the Exodus. Divide your class into teams and give each a set of cards which you have prepared. Each card has one part of the Joseph story. Give it to the children out of order and the teams' task is to put them in sequence. Prizes can be given to the first group that is successful. Then ask if there is a card that can be eliminated but still have the story end up the same way. (This would be a good exercise for younger children to do at a *Seder*.)

King Solomon and the Queen of Sheba

By Blu Greenberg and Linda Tarry
Illustrated by Avi Katz
Pitspopany Press, 1997
48 pages
ISBN 0-943706-90-4
Grades 2-4

This charmingly written and illustrated book tells the stories of Solomon as a youth and then as king of Israel, and of Makeda as a girl and then as queen of Sheba. It is told in several quickly read chapters, and covers many important facets of Jewish history, such as the building of the First Temple and the origin of the Ethiopian Jews. In addition to all the information included, it is also a poignant love story of two rulers who met, wed, loved, and ultimately had to live apart to rule their separate nations.

Main Ideas

- Solomon and Makeda had interesting lives.

- According to legend, Ethiopian Jewry began with the marriage of Solomon and Makeda.

- Leadership involves difficult responsibilities.

Discussion Starters

- Do you think King Abera chose the correct child to be his successor? Why?

- Which riddle that Makeda asked Solomon did you think was the hardest, and why?

- Did you feel Makeda and Solomon *had* to separate?

Activities

? Working in small groups or individually come up with your own riddles. The best one wins a prize (maybe a book of riddles!).

Turn this story into a play and perform it for the parents of the children in your school or youth group.

 For a taste of Ethiopian food, make *Dabo*, an Ethiopian Sabbath Bread:

1 tsp. dry yeast
2 tbs. baking powder
3 C. water; lukewarm
2 egg yolks
1 tsp. salt
1 tbs. sugar
1 tbs. corn oil
4 C. flour

1. In mixing bowl, dissolve dry yeast and baking powder in the water.
2. Mix in egg yolks, salt, sugar, and oil.
3. Add the flour and prepare a smooth dough by kneading for 5 minutes.
4. Let dough rise in a covered bowl at room temperature for about 6 hours. Punch down.
5. In lightly oiled large round skillet, place the dough.
6. Cover pan and let dough rise for 1 hour.
7. Cook it, still covered, over gas or electricity on the top of the stove at low heat for 25-30 minutes.
8. Turn the loaf over and bake on the other side 5 minutes more.
9. Serve at room temperature.

The Book of Tens

Written and illustrated by Mark Podwal
Greenwillow Books, 1994
24 pages
ISBN 0-688-12994-3
Grades 4-6

This book explores the sacred significance of the number 10 and its many appearances in the Bible. In his introduction, Podwal claims that "Ten appears and reappears so frequently in the Holy Scriptures that the story of the Bible can almost be retold by means of its citings." Each of his 21 entries gives succinct background information and is accompanied by an evocative, sometimes whimsical, gouache and ink illustration. The book pulls from Bible, Talmud, Midrash, and legends, but does not give citations.

Main Ideas

- Ten is a significant number in the Bible.
- Talmud, Midrash, and legend often provide imaginative explanations of biblical passages.
- There are many different sources that can be used when studying the Bible.

Discussion Starters

- What other numbers besides 10 have Jewish significance? Which numbers are significant for you? Why?
- Why do you think God spoke to no one in the ten generations between Adam and Noah? between Noah and Abraham?
- "Ten spies falsely reported that the Promised Land was filled with giants." Why would they tell such a story?

Activities

 List all of Podwal's 21 mentions of the number 10 on a piece of paper and duplicate the paper. Divide your class into study pairs. Have the pairs number the entries from least important to most important and have them present their reasoning to the class. Keep a tally of the answers on a big piece of newsprint or on the chalkboard.

 Mix up the study pairs and have each pick out of a bag one of the instances of the number 10 mentioned in the book. Have them plan part of a mural that will have their number 10 depicted on it. Provide a mural-sized piece of craft paper to each pair, along with paints, brushes, and markers and have them illustrate their idea. Use rafia to bind the pieces together to hang on the walls of the synagogue. If space is an issue, give the children 17" x 11" pieces of craft paper to do the same, but bind these sheets into a book for display.

This book provides a great opportunity to teach your children about many different sacred writings of the Jewish people. For each explanation given for a particular number 10, clarify where the idea came from. Show the books and explain how they relate to each other.

King Solomon and His Magic Ring

By Elie Wiesel
Illustrated by Mark Podwal
Greenwillow Books, 1999
56 pages
ISBN 0-688-16959-7
Grades 4-6

The biblical and legendary accounts of King Solomon, the third king of Israel, are loosely woven together in this simple and elegant book. Wiesel has included stories of wisdom, of love, of demons, of angels, and of unimaginable beauty. It's chatty style makes it ideal for reading aloud. The text is accompanied by full-color art.

Main Ideas

- King Solomon was a king of Israel.
- There are many stories about King Solomon.
- King Solomon's wisdom is legendary.

Discussion Starters

- It is said that King Solomon's ring was engraved with three Hebrew words, גַּם זֶה יַעֲבֹר (gam zeh ya'avor) meaning "This, too, shall pass." Why would these words bring comfort to someone who is sad, and sadness to someone who is happy?

- God told Solomon, "I will grant you whatever you wish." Solomon asked only for wisdom. If you knew you would be granted whatever you requested, for what would you wish?

- Solomon caught a bird in a boastful lie. When the bird was accused of wrongdoing, it said, "Have you forgotten that one says all kinds of foolish things to impress one's beloved?" Do you think there are times when it is all right to lie? to stretch the truth?

Activities

 Have each child select one of the vignettes presented in this book and research and read its source(s). Have source books available and marked, including Kings I, *The Book of Legends* by H.N. Bialik and Y.H. Ravnitsky, and *The Legends of the Jews* by Louis Ginzberg. Depending on their ability, students may need help reading these texts. Then have each child write his or her own version of the story.

 Give each child a dime-store ring, the kind that is given as prizes at Purim carnivals. Have each one decide and then describe for the class what special power it has. List these powers on the board with students' names. When everyone has had a turn, see if anyone wants to trade rings. Continue the trading for a certain period of time or until everyone is satisfied.

 Read again the passages about demons in these stories. Give children drawing paper, and pencils and tell each to choose two colored crayons. Then, have them draw what they think a demon might look like.

But God Remembered: Stories of Women from Creation To the Promised Land

By Sandy Eisenberg Sasso
Illustrated by Bethanne Andersen
Jewish Lights Publishing, 1995
32 pages
ISBN 1-879045-43-5
Grades 6-8

This is a unique collection of four different stories about biblical women who are mentioned only briefly in the Torah. The very first woman, Pharaoh's daughter, Jacob's granddaughter, and the daughters of Zelophehad are each given life in these Midrashim. In each case, Rabbi Sasso starts with the biblical text, then weaves a story from it. The book is prefaced with a little story on forgetfulness and remembering.

Main Ideas

- There are few stories in the Bible about women.
- Midrashim flesh out these stories.
- People often forget, but God remembers.

Discussion Starters

- God says to Lilith and to Adam: "This is something only you can do." What is meant by this? Can an intermediary help with some conflicts? What kind?

- In the story of Serach bat Asher, music plays an important role. Think about the kinds of music to which you like to listen. What can music do to/for people?

- The preface of this book has a short story about forgetfulness and remembering. God says, "There are some things people will need to forget." What kinds of things? Explain.

Activities

 Serach sings of Abraham, Isaac, Sarah, Rebekkah, Hagar, Ishmael, Esau, Jacob, and his 12 sons and his daughter Dinah. Using Genesis, chart a family tree from Abraham to the grandchildren of Jacob.

 "The Daughters of Z" is a good story to act out, either as a biblical story or as a modern story. Appoint a narrator and assign the roles of the daughters, three Judges, Moses, God's voice, and tribesmen of Manasseh. Students can use the dialogue in the book or improvise to expand the story. Or, they can act out the play on the subject in *Sedra Scenes: Skits for Every Torah Portion* by Stan J. Beiner (A.R.E. Publishing, Inc., 1982), pp. 184-187, or in *Parashah Plays: For Children of All Ages* by Richard J. Allen (A.R.E. Publishing, Inc., 2000), pp. 252-259.

 Make up sets of "tribal cards" with a name and symbol of one tribe per card. Split class into two or three teams and play *Tribal Pursuits*. First, a player on each team is given a physical task to accomplish, for example: 30 jumping jacks in 30 seconds. If successful, they earn a question which you can construct from the stories in this book. If they answer correctly, the team receives one tribal card. The first team to collect all 12 tribal cards wins.

Miriam

By Beatrice Gormley
Eerdmans Books for Young Readers, 1999
192 pages
ISBN 0-8028-5156-8
Grades 6-8

READ ALONE

This historical/biblical novel is told from the point of view of Moses' sister Miriam and of Nebet, the chief lady-in-waiting to Bint-Anath, the Egyptian princess who adopted Moses. It spans only a few years, from right before Moses' conception until he is about two and a half years old. However, much of his story is told through the visions Miriam has of his future and the future of the Hebrews in Egypt. Miriam's role is central in this version, and it is refreshing to have a Jewish heroine developed and explained in such a positive and insightful manner.

Main Ideas

- Moses had a relationship with his family of origin and with his adopted Egyptian royal family.
- The Jewish people's slavery in Egypt had a historical perspective.
- Miriam struggled with accepting her role as a leader

Discussion Starters

- Who is your favorite character in this book and why?
- What was most interesting to you about this book's descriptions of life in the village and in the palace? Explain your answer.
- Do you feel Miriam made the "right" decision at the end of the book by returning to her village instead of following Nebet's plan? (Try to put the rest of the story (which we all know) out of your mind when answering this question.)

Activities

 Make a Miriam's Cup in honor of Miriam for your family to have and to use at your next Pesach *Seder*. Write a short poem about Miriam that can be put on the cup or recited when using the cup at the *Seder*.

 Pick another famous biblical girl or woman and write a short story from her point of view.

 Read about Miriam in Exodus 2:1-10 and Exodus 15:20-21. See if this book deviates from the biblical accounts. Compare and contrast the book with the biblical passages.

Escape from Egypt

By Sonia Levitin
Penguin, 1996
267 pages
ISBN 0-14-037537-6
Grades 9-12

READ ALONE

In this novel, the most famous travel tale of our history — the Exodus from Egypt — is told in a way that makes it seem real, believable, and vividly present. Teenagers will relate to the passionate and hormone-driven relationship between Jesse, the young Hebrew slave, and Jennat, the beautiful half-Egyptian and half-Syrian servant in a rich Egyptian household. Their personal love story, filled with pain, longing, anguish, separations, and ultimate happiness is set against the backdrop of Moses coming to lead his people out of Egypt. This story is seen through the various characters, Egyptians and Hebrews, and their sufferings during the plagues that affected the entire land of Egypt, and during the travails of the journey out of Egypt. It evokes a genuine tale that you will realize could really have happened — and how horrible, yet exciting, those times were!

Main Ideas

- When the Jewish people left Egypt, it was a monumental undertaking.

- The development of faith in the Jewish people through their Exodus was an important occurrence.

- The love of God and of human beings is of utmost importance.

Discussion Starters

- What part of the Hebrew slavery experience horrified you the most? What part of the servant's experience in In-hop-tep's household was the worst?

- Which plague (besides the last and, of course, the worst) seemed to be the most horrific, and why? Can you think of a plague that God did not use, but might have?

Why didn't Jesse also marry Talia? Should he have followed his heart and married Jennat, or done as Rishon wanted and married Talia for the good of his family?

Activities

 This book makes the story of Exodus real. With your group or class, develop something to incorporate into your *Seder* that will give the same realistic effect. For example, using props, demonstrate each plague.

 Slavery still exists in parts of our world today. Research this horrific fact and do something meaningful about it: lobby an elected official, raise money to donate to an organization fighting slavery, write letters to local newspapers, etc.

 Pick your favorite character from the book and appear at your *Seder* as that character. Try to remain in character for the entire meal. This will be sure to enliven the experience for all who attend!

For Further Reading

PK

Bible Heroes I Can Be by Ann Eisenberg, illustrated by Rosalyn Schanzer. Kar-Ben Copies, Inc., 1990. 20 pages. ISBN 0-929371-09-7.

> This is a charming introduction for very young children to the attributes of famous biblical characters. It also shows how a small child can possess these same attributes. Those characters featured are Noah, Abraham and Sara, Rebecca, Joseph, Miriam and Moses, Joshua, Ruth and Naomi, King David, and King Solomon.

Why the Moon Only Glows by Dina Rosenfeld, illustrated by Yehudit Holtzman. Hachai Publishing, 1992. 28 pages. ISBN 0-92261-300-1.

> In this picture book, a father tells his children the Midrash of why the sun shines but the moon only glows. He explains that on the fourth day of creation, the two great lights are created, but the moon complains to God. The moon asserts that one of them should be bigger and brighter and — of course — the boastful moon thinks that it should be biggest. God decides to use this request as a lesson in humility, making the moon the lesser of the lights. However, after punishing the moon, God shows mercy, and the moon is given a sky full of stars to help him. Told in verse, this is a lovely bedtime story.

Grades K-3

Does God Have a Big Toe? Stories about Stories in the Bible by Marc Gellman, illustrated by Oscar de Mejo. HarperCollins Children's Books, 1989. 88 pages. ISBN 0-06-022432-0.

> This is a collection of short, humorous stories derived from Torah that ask, as well as answer, questions. The last tale, "The Announcing Tool," is perfect to read before the High Holy Days. All the stories are great fun to read aloud.

The Shadow of a Flying Bird: A Folklore from the Kurdistan retold and illustrated by Mordicai Gerstein. Hyperion Books for Children, 1994. 32 pages. ISBN 0-7868-0016-X.

> This is a retelling of a Midrash from the Kurdistani Jews in which Moses, at the end of his life, refuses to give up his soul to God, who is forced to take it with a single kiss. It expresses the love that Moses had for life and that God has for Moses. (You will want to review illustrations and be sure your children are old enough to handle some of the frightening images.)

Ten Classic Jewish Children's Stories retold by Peninnah Schram, illustrated by Jeffrey Allon. Pitspopany Press, 1998. 48 pages. ISBN 0-943706-96-3.

Master storyteller Peninnah Schram has taken stories from the written and oral traditions of the Jews and presented them for children, accompanied by questions to consider. The questions are designed to help children explore the different values and traditions introduced in the stories.

Grades 2-4

The Angel and the Donkey retold by Katherine Paterson and illustrated by Alexander Koshkin. Clarion Books, 1996. 32 pages. ISBN 0-395-68969-4.

This is the biblical story of Balaam the soothsayer; his faithful donkey; Balak, the king of Moab; and the wandering Jews led by Moses. It has been clearly recounted, beautifully illustrated, and would make a good additional reading for Passover and the story of the Exodus.

Moses retold and illustrated by Leonard Everett Fisher. Holiday House, 1995. 32 pages. ISBN 0-8234-1149-0.

This is a lavishly and dramatically illustrated rendition of the Exodus story. The language is mostly formal and therefore is not suitable for younger children, although the adult reader could change the wording to suit a listener's abilities. The story begins with the hiding of Moses and ends with his death and the Israelites crossing the river Jordan. Unfortunately, aside from watching over her baby brother until he is found, Miriam's role is ignored. Also given are the family tree of Moses and a map of the journey from Goshen to Jericho.

Grades 4-6

Before There Was a Before by Arthur, David, and Shoshana Waskow, illustrated by Amnon Danziger. Adama Books, 1984. 88 pages. ISBN 0-915361-08-6.

In this book, Arthur Waskow and his two children give the classic story of creation many new twists. The black and white illustrations starkly contrast with the flowing language of the book and provide a very interesting counterbalance. Creation is explained from God's point of view and through conversations God has with the world and with people. This book is remarkable in its unique transformation of a well-known and often repeated and studied story.

God's Mailbox by Marc Gellman, illustrated by Debbie Tilley. Morrow Junior Books, 1996. 111 pages. ISBN 0-688-13169-7.

This book is comprised of 18 Midrashim, each uniquely thought provoking, meaningful, and containing important life lessons. Each one illuminates some aspect of the Bible in an easy to understand way and would make an excellent discussion starter for any group studying Bible, ethics, or *mitzvot*.

Moses and the Angels by Ileene Smith Sobel, illustrated by Mark Podwal, with an introduction by Elie Wiesel. Bantam Doubleday Dell Publishing Group, Inc., 1999. 64 pages. ISBN 0-385-32612-2.

> This is a beautifully illustrated collection of Midrashim about the life of Moses and the angels who act as his protectors throughout his 120 years. These stories can be read along with the Torah passages they explore.

Grades 6-8

Clouds of Glory by Miriam Chaikin, woodcuts by David Frampton. Clarion Books, 1998. 118 pages. ISBN 0-395-74654-X.

> These 21 stories are strung together as a narrative about God's relationship with creation. Its scope is from the second day of creation to the binding of Isaac and includes a female as well as a male perspective. Many points are raised that would make excellent discussion starters. Chaikin provides notes that explain which part of each story is Bible and which part legend. Her sources are Rashi, *Legends of the Bible* by Louis Ginzberg, and *Gates to the Old City* by Raphael Patai.

David: A Biography by Barbara Cohen, illustrated by David Frampton. Clarion Books, 1995. 108 pages. ISBN 0-395-58702-6.

> Barbara Cohen tells the biography of one of the most famous leaders in all of Jewish history. In modern language, she describes David as a man, poet, soldier, politician, administrator, lover, father, and religious leader. This is not a religious tract that speaks of God working through David, but rather presents the two of them in a type of partnership. A particularly good feature of this book is the extensive bibliography included at the end.

When the Beginning Began: Stories about God, the Creatures, and Us by Julius Lester, illustrated by Emily Lisker. Silver Whistle, a registered trademark of Harcourt Brace & Company, 1999. 112 pages. ISBN 0-15-201238-9.

> Written especially for skeptics who might not make their way to the stories of the Bible otherwise, this book of 17 stories includes tales that are sometimes funny, sometimes serious, sometimes troubling, but always creative. Julius Lester is a master storyteller who has let his imagination loose in the retelling of these stories of Creation. Lester uses a variety of images for God — male, female, bird, a mountain, rose petals, and other things as well.

Grades 9-12

Be Not Far from Me: The Oldest Love Story — Legends from the Bible retold by Eric A. Kimmel, illustrated by David Diaz. Simon & Schuster Books for Young Readers, 1998. 256 pages. ISBN 0-689-81088-1.

Kimmel has powerfully retold stories of biblical heroes and heroines, including stories from the Prophets. The stories begin with Abram (Abraham) and end with Daniel. The book includes a note on sources, maps, and a time line. This is a wonderful companion to reading the stories in Torah and Prophets.

Listen To Her Voice: Women of the Hebrew Bible by Miki Raver, accompanied by classic works of art. Chronicle Books, 1998. 175 pages. ISBN 0-8118-1895-0.

The lives of 18 women from the Bible are explored in this sumptuous combination of Bible text, Rabbinic and modern scholarship, and magnificent art work.

The Red Tent by Anita Diamant. St. Martins Press, 1997. 320 pages. ISBN 0-312-16978-7.

At last, Dinah, Jacob's only daughter, gets to tell her story against a vividly drawn description of biblical life. It is a compelling fictionalized narrative which celebrates the lives of our matriarchs and passes their stories on to us. Reading this book will provide an opportunity to review the biblical stories of our mothers and fathers from a woman's point of view.

All Ages

The Bird of Paradise and Other Sabbath Stories by Steven M. Rosman, illustrated by Joel Iskowitz. UAHC Press, 1994. 176 pages. ISBN 0-8074-0529-9.

Here is a collection of Jewish stories, including original tales and adaptations from Midrash, the Talmud, and the Hasidic masters. The illustrations are minimal and the source notes sparse, but the stories are perfect accompaniments to the weekly Torah portions.

God's Story: How God Made Mankind by Jan Mark, illustrated by David Parkins. Candlewick Press, 1997. 179 pages. ISBN 0-7636-0376-7.

Jan Mark has drawn on ancient Midrashim to write an easily understood narrative of the Tanach. What emerges is the portrait of a God struggling to be at one with humankind, a God who thinks and speaks and suffers.

The Kids' Catalog of Bible Treasures written and illustrated by Chaya M. Burstein. The Jewish Publication Society, 1999. 142 pages. ISBN 0-8276-0667-2.

This is a fabulous source book filled with information and activities covering the Tanach, Talmud, Mishnah, Responsa, and more.

Chapter 2

Ethics: Doing the Right Thing

During our lives, we are called upon to make many choices. Sometimes we make "right" choices and sometimes we don't. Sue's father recently reminded her of the famous saying: "The measure of a person's character is what that person would do if no one could see what he or she was doing." This is very true, and each of us struggles daily with doing what we know and feel to be the correct thing. Sometimes we even succeed.

These books are all about life choices and the tools we can use as we face difficult decisions. It is hoped that sharing them with children will enable them to incorporate these tools into their daily lives.

Featured Books

The Secret Room (PK)
Ten Good Rules (PK)
The Giving Tree (K-3)
The Kingdom of the Singing Birds (K-3)
Mrs. Katz and Tush (K-3)
What Zeesie Saw on Delancey Street (K-3)
The Christmas Menorahs (4-6)
Who Knows Ten? (4-6)
Unfinished Dreams (6-8)
The Violin Players (6-8)
In My Hands (9-12)
Tuesdays with Morrie (9-12)

The Secret Room

Written and illustrated by Uri Shulevitz
Farrar Straus Giroux, 1993
32 pages
ISBN 0-374-46596-7
PK

This clever little story tells of the meeting of a king and a man whose head was gray and whose beard was black. Because of his wisdom and innate goodness, this man becomes the king's treasurer and then the king's chief counselor. The illustrations are quite charming, bold, and bright.

Main Ideas

- Honesty pays.
- Greed can cause a lot of trouble.
- Wisdom is better than possessions.

Discussion Starters

- Did you think that the man's response to the king about why his head was gray and beard black was a clever answer?
- Were you surprised at what was in the secret room? Do you have a secret place?
- Which character did you like best, and why?

Activities

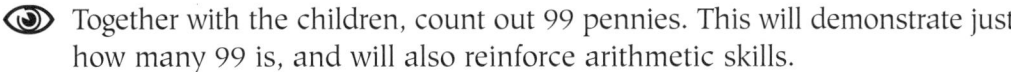 Together with the children, count out 99 pennies. This will demonstrate just how many 99 is, and will also reinforce arithmetic skills.

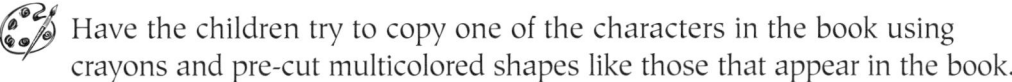 Have the children try to copy one of the characters in the book using crayons and pre-cut multicolored shapes like those that appear in the book.

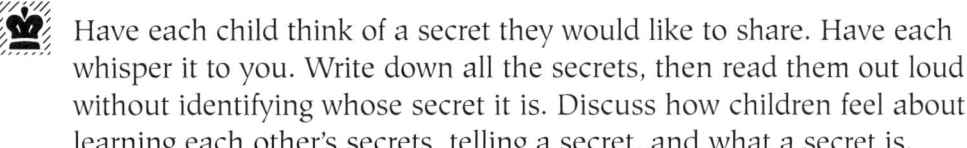 Have each child think of a secret they would like to share. Have each whisper it to you. Write down all the secrets, then read them out loud without identifying whose secret it is. Discuss how children feel about learning each other's secrets, telling a secret, and what a secret is.

Ten Good Rules

By Susan Remick Topek
Illustrated by Rosalyn Schanzer
Kar-Ben Copies, Inc., 1991
32 pages
ISBN 0-929371-28-3
PK

READ ALOUD

Here is a simple restatement of the Ten Commandments intended for very young children. To reinforce counting, a little figure of Moses in a child's hand holds up the appropriate number of fingers for each of the good rules. In some instances, the commandments are recast from negative to positive language.

Main Ideas

- God gave people ten good rules by which to live.
- The Israelites promised to follow these rules.
- These rules are still important today.

Discussion Starters

- After reading each commandment, ask the children what it means.
- What can we do to follow or "listen" to each rule?
- Which do you think is the most important rule for you right now?

Activities

 Give each child a cut-out of the tablets big enough to incorporate a tracing of a child's hand. Help children trace their hands onto the tablets and give them crayons and small stickers with which to decorate the tracings.

 Combining the fourth and fifth rule, have each child make a Shabbat present for their parents. Here is one idea. Make plaster wall plaques (see *Kids Create! Art & Craft Experiences for 3-To-9-Year-Olds* by Laurie Carlson, Williamson Publishing, 1990). Use a coffee can lid and pour in plaster of paris as per directions on the box. Have each child press his/her hand firmly and without wiggling into the plaster, then carefully remove it. Before the plaster hardens, stick a large paper clip into the top so the plaque can be hung from a picture hook. When the plaster has dried, remove it from the lid. Have each child paint his/her handprint with gold paint. Be sure to mark each plaque with the maker's name and the date. (Note: use buckets of water to rinse hands and lids. Avoid pouring the plaster down the sink. Instead, empty the buckets outside.)

 Put each letter of the name "Moses" on a large piece of cardboard. Using the tune of the song "Bingo," sing: "He brought ten rules from Mt. Sinai and Moses was his name, oh . . . . M-O-S-E-S, M-O-S-E-S, M-O-S-E-S and Moses was his name, oh!" Each time you sing this, remove a letter from the end of "Moses" and substitute a clap.

The Giving Tree

Written and illustrated by Shel Silverstein
HarperCollins Publishers, 1964
54 pages
ISBN 0–6-025665-6
K-3

READ ALOUD

READ ALONE

READ TOGETHER

This book is one of those classics that lasts throughout the ages. We can all learn something wonderful and hopeful from the steadfast devotion and love that the tree in this tale has for its "little" boy.

Main Ideas

- Love and friendship are important.
- Giving your all to another is one way of loving.
- Time passes and people grow up.

Discussion Starters

- Do you think the tree was right or wrong to give everything it had, and was, to the boy? Why?
- What about the boy? Was he nice to the tree? Was he a true friend?
- Have you ever given something away to someone you really like? How did you feel when you did?

Activities

 Talk about the meaning of the word *"tzedakah,"* then come up with an age appropriate *tzedakah* project. For example, have your students bring a penny to every class. With the pennies, buy a plant and together bring it to a local resident in a nursing home.

 Go for a nature walk with your class and try to find as many different kinds of trees as you can.

 Ask the children to list all the people who give things to them. Help each child to make a thank-you note for one special person.

The Kingdom of Singing Birds

By Miriam Aroner
Illustrated by Shelly O. Haas
Kar-Ben Copies, Inc., 1993
28 Pages
ISBN 0-929371-43-7
K-3

This lovely fable about the gentle Rabbi Zusya and his simplistic wisdom has equally lovely pale pastel artwork which complements it perfectly. This story is all about setting something free and having it be able to reach its full potential. In this story, this happens with the birds that did not sing until they were set free and given the choice to stay or leave.

Main Ideas

- Freedom is the most important thing to living beings.

- Even a simple person has something to teach the most powerful person.

- Giving a choice to someone may get you what you want from them.

Discussion Starters

- What did you think was the most interesting of Zusya's questions? Explain your answer.

- Why do you think the birds did not sing until they were let free? What is so important about being free that enables one to do something not possible before?

- If you were Zusya, what would you want your reward to be, and how would you use it?

Activities

 Have the children look at all the pictures of the birds in this book, as well as birds in some other bird books. Have them pick their favorite one to draw and decorate. Supply glitter, feathers, cut up material, stickers, etc.

 Brainstorm things the children in the class can do because they are free. Then brainstorm a second list of all the things that they would be unable to do if they were not free. In a discussion, compare the two lists.

Have children think of something they could do that would "free" up another person in their lives (e.g., doing a chore for a parent). Discuss the things they thought about. Then, perhaps they may even be willing to carry out their ideas.

Mrs. Katz and Tush

Written and illustrated by Patricia Polacco
A Bantam Little Rooster Book, 1992
30 pages
ISBN 0-553-08122-5
K-3

A young African American boy, Larnel, and his family befriend a lonely, widowed, elderly Jewish neighbor. Their relationship deepens when Larnel gives her a kitten and when he begins to learn from her about the commonalities of the Jewish and African-American experiences of slavery. Larnel and the neighbor begin to celebrate holidays together, and their friendship deepens until her death.

Main Ideas

- Intergenerational friendships can be very meaningful.

- There is a commonality of suffering.

- Pesach is an important Jewish holiday.

Discussion Starters

- Do you have a special friend who is much older or younger than you? Who is it? How did you become friends?

- What was the one thing that really caused Larnel and Mrs. Katz to become friends?

- Who contributed more to the friendship of Larnel and Mrs. Katz — Larnel's mother or Tush?

Activities

 Bring a special older/younger friend to class and do a joint project together about friendship. One idea is to make friendship bracelets.

 Discuss what freedom means. Make a list for each child to take home and post to help them and their family appreciate the freedom they live with daily and often take for granted.

Talk about loneliness and help students think of something special they can do for someone they think might be lonely.

What Zeesie Saw on Delancey Street

By Elsa Okon Rael
Illustrated by Marjorie Priceman
Simon & Schuster Books for Young Readers, 1996
32 pages
ISBN 0-689-80549-7
K-3

READ ALOUD

This outstanding book evokes the immigrant experience of the early 1900s on the Lower East Side of Manhattan, while delivering a powerful message of community and charity. The heroine of the story is Zeesie, a seven-year-old Jewish girl. She is allowed to attend her first "package party," an event to raise money to bring more people over from "the old country." Zeesie's father tells her about the money room — a place where the men go one by one either to leave money if they can afford it or to take it if they need it. Zeesie's curiosity brings her to the room where she hides and witnesses her father's friend taking money. It is a secret she must keep to herself.

Main Ideas

- Charity can be anonymous.
- It is important to be able to receive when you have need.
- People in a community take care of each other.

Discussion Starters

- Who are the people in your community? (Have children think about different communities to which they belong, e.g., synagogue, family, school, neighborhood.)

- What kinds of things can people in a community do for each other?

- Why is it important to give money to those who need it? Why is it important to be able to receive money if you are in need? Why do you think it is important that Zeesie not tell anyone what she saw?

Activities

 Identify a needy group in your community and have your class raise whatever money it can to help. Make a simple, modest money box, then ask the children to bring in pennies and nickels from their allowance. While you may collect only a few dollars over several months, the money will be an important gift from the children themselves.

 Zeesie and her parents walk to the party through the streets of the Lower East Side. Help children draw a map of your synagogue (or meeting place) on a mural-sized piece of craft paper. Identify all the different areas in the building. Have children cut out shapes and pictures from magazines that represent different things in the building, then paste them onto the "map."

 Play some Yiddish music and let the children dance. Provide refreshments and make it a party.

The Christmas Menorahs: How a Town Fought Hate

By Janice Cohn
Illustrated by Bill Farnsworth
Albert Whitman & Company, 2000
40 pages
ISBN 0-8075-1153-6
Grades 4-6

This true story begins when a rock is thrown through the bedroom window of a Jewish boy in Billings, Montana. Because a *chanukiah*, a Chanukah *menorah*, was displayed in his window, he became a target for this hate crime. The town's response to the incident makes this a remarkable and uplifting book. After hearing about the incident, many non-Jewish residents displayed a *menorah* in their homes as a show of support and solidarity for their Jewish neighbors and as a weapon against bigotry. This book is an effective way of showing that "hate can make a lot of noise. Love and courage are usually quieter. But in the end, they're the strongest."

Main Ideas

- Fighting bigotry is important.
- Religious freedom is important now, just as it was in the past for the Maccabees.
- Friendship has power in the face of hate.

Discussion Starters

- Have you ever experienced bigotry or prejudice? When and where? Did you ever feel uncomfortable about being Jewish or displaying Jewish symbols in your house?

- Can you understand why Isaac did not want to be a pioneer? Can you understand why he told his friends that his Chanukah presents were Christmas presents? Why do kids want so much to be like everyone else that they might tell a lie?

- Do you think that such a hate crime could happen in the town in which you live? Would the response of the majority of your neighbors be the same as it was in Billings? Explain your answer.

Activities

Invite a local Christian youth group/religious class to your meeting place/synagogue. Organize a joint activity, as well as a discussion of perceptions of each other's similarities and differences. Then facilitate a discussion about religious freedom, how both groups practice their religions, and discuss any bigotry they may have experienced. Have participants think of ways to combat the bigotry.

From your local newspaper, pick out some articles about recent hate crime attacks. (Unfortunately, these probably won't be too difficult to find.) Discuss with students how they feel about these crimes and what, if anything, they can do about them. One idea is for each student to write a letter to the editor of the newspaper expressing his/her views on a particular crime. Another is to do something supportive for the victim.

Remember that this can be an upsetting and troubling book to some of your students. Focus on the positives that came out of the terrible crime and talk with them about other positives that have occurred during terrible times. A good source is the book *Rescuers: Portraits in Moral Courage* by Malka Drucker and Gay Block, Holmes & Meier Publishers, Inc., 1992.

Who Knows Ten? Children's Tales of the Ten Commandments

By Molly Cone
Illustrated by Robin Brickman
UAHC Press, 1997 (revised edition)
112 pages
ISBN 0-8074-0080-7
Grades 4-6

Originally published in 1965, *Who Knows Ten* has continued to be a favorite of parents, teachers, and children. Molly Cone has chosen stories from the Talmud and Jewish folklore to elucidate each of the Ten Commandments, and she has chosen well. The book helps children learn "how to do justice and what is good."

Main Ideas

- After the Israelites heard the Ten Commandments, they said, *"Na'aseh v'nishma"* — We will do and we will listen (Exodus 24:7).

- Each commandment has layers of meaning.

- The commandments are a guide to doing justice and good.

Discussion Starters

- This book contains ten different stories. Which is your favorite, and why? How does the story apply to your own life?

- In the story "The Gossip," the woman says, "It's not like I can't take back what I said." Do you think it is possible to take back hurtful words? Did you ever say something you wish you hadn't? Did anyone ever say something to you that still hurts when you remember it?

- Do you think one commandment is more important than all the others? If so, which one, and why?

Activities

 Divide students into groups of five or six, then have each group select a story from the book they would like to act out. Present these playlets for the rest of the group or for parents or other classes.

 Ask each student to pick one of the Ten Commandments and write a few sentences about why it is important to him/her. Then compare and discuss the writings.

 Bake, decorate, and eat "Ten Commandments cookies." You can make this into a contest giving the winner the extra cookies. Shavuot is the perfect holiday for this activity.

Directions:
1. Have children roll out and cut refrigerated cookie dough into the shape of the tablets.
2. Bake according to the directions on the package and let the cookies cool.
3. Decorate the cookies using tubes of blue and white cake icing, then eat them.

Unfinished Dreams: A Novel

By Jane Breskin Zalben
Simon & Schuster Books for Young Readers, 1996
164 pages
ISBN 0-689-80033-9
Grades 6-8

READ ALONE

Jason Grass, a sixth grader, is faced with a series of losses that keeps him thinking and growing. His mentor and principal, Mr. Carr, has contracted HIV. The reaction in the community is anger, fear, and grief. The subject of AIDS and homosexuality is handled sensitively, and within the context of tolerance for differences. (In one chapter, some basic sex education is delivered by the coach.)

Main Ideas

- It takes more courage to be different than to be the same.
- Adults can't always fix things.
- It's who you are on the inside and what you do that matters.

Discussion Starters

- While talking about what it was like when his father died, Jason's father says, "It's the person inside that comes out through the little things they do and don't do. You can't always listen to what people say. It's what they *do* in life . . . talk is cheap." Can you remember a time when somebody said they would do something, but didn't follow through? Describe your feelings when this happened.

- After Jason's violin is destroyed, he thinks about how hard it is to know someone. What do you think it would take to know someone else truly?

- Jason's mother says: "I think that we all make choices about the paths we decide to take . . . Even though I believe in choices, there's a corner of my heart that also believes in fate." Which do you think plays more of a part in life — our own wisdom in making our choices, or just plain luck?

Activities

 In the beginning of the school year, have your group make individual wish lists as Jason's teacher does. Then instruct each student to check his/her list every few months and decide if he or she would change it. This activity is intended for private reflection, not for class sharing.

 As a group, make a time capsule containing items that the class members think are important. Secure it somewhere in your building with a note explaining that it is to be opened by the students at the end of the year. During the last class session, open the box. See if they would choose differently now, or simply discuss the contents of the capsule and why the children chose the items in it.

 At the end of the book, Mr. Carr gives Jason seven pieces of advice. Have each child go to an elder in their family and ask for seven pieces of advice. Have them share what they have been told, and look for similarities in the pieces of advice.

The Violin Players

By Eileen Bluestone Sherman
The Jewish Publication Society, 1998
121 pages
ISBN 0-8276-0595-1
Grades 6-8

When Melissa Jensen's father takes a temporary position at a Midwestern college, Melissa learns what it means to be Jewish. Compared to being one of many Jews in New York City, it is quite different being one of two Jewish students at her new high school. Melissa witnesses anti-Semitism in subtle and not so subtle episodes, but remains silent. As she ponders the situation, she wonders about what it really means to be Jewish, and begins a journey to find out.

Main Ideas

 Ignorance of one's own religion can lead to problems.

 Anti-Semitism presents itself in many different ways.

 It is important to confront hatred.

Discussion Starters

- Melissa's grandmother says, "Ignorance, Melissa, is a terrible, terrible curse . . ." What do you think she meant by this? Can you think of any examples in the book in which this is illustrated?

- When someone paints "Jew Lover" in Rob's locker, Rob and Daniel wash it off and don't tell anyone. What would you do?

- Johnny is very open about his bigotry. Kathy is indifferent. Do you think one is worse than the other? Why or why not?

Activities

📖 Read the story of Purim. Discuss why Melissa thinks that if she had known this story, she would have known better how to handle the situation in which she finds herself.

🎵 Music, especially violin playing, is important to Melissa and Daniel. Playing the instrument is very difficult. Have your group listen to some violin music, or watch a videotape of Itzhak Perlman. Have students research the many Jews who are or were famous classical violin players (e.g., Yehudi Menuhin, Jascha Heifetz, Isaac Stern, Gil Shaham, Pinchas Zuckerman, Nathan Milstein, Shlomo Mintz).

📄 Make contact with students at a synagogue in another part of the country. Have your class write to them to learn what it is like to be Jewish in their city. Then compare their lifestyle and resources with those of your city.

In My Hands: Memories of a Holocaust Rescuer

By Irene Gut Opdyke with Jennifer Armstrong
Alfred A. Knopf, Inc., 1999
280 pages
ISBN 0-679-89181-1
Grades 9-12

READ ALONE

This wonderful memoir of an extraordinary woman is a shining example of good choices made under the worst of all possible conditions. Irene makes her innate goodness and compassion seem ordinary and the only possible way to behave. Her resistance to the German oppression of Poland and the Jewish people during World War II is inspiring and uplifting. It is an important part of Holocaust education, and also life education to teach students that during the Holocaust there were many "Righteous Gentiles."

Main Ideas

- There are people of good will even during the worst of times.
- Morality can sometimes win over immorality.
- There are positive lessons we can learn from the Holocaust.

Discussion Starters

- Why would the priest refuse to give Irene absolution? How could he take that position? Can you make an argument in support of his position?
- What was it that made Irene such a caring and thoughtful person who risked her life for others?
- Other than Irene, who do you admire in this book? Explain your answer.

Activities

 The Milgram experiment was conducted in the 1960s as a way to measure people's compliance with authority. Have students research it in an encyclopedia or on the Internet. Compare and contrast the results of this experiment with the compliance of so many Poles with the Germans during World War II. (Note: Remember that Irene herself was seen by others as a willing prostitute of the Nazis.)

 Ask a local survivor or righteous gentile to talk with your class or group about the issue of choice. Call your local Jewish Federation office for names.

 To show gratitude to Irene, ask each student to choose one lesson he/she can distill from this book, then write a short essay on what it means to them. Mail the essays to Irene Gut Opdyke, c/o Alfred A. Knopf, Inc., 299 Park Ave., New York, NY 10170.

Tuesdays with Morrie

By Mitch Albom
Doubleday, 1997
192 pages
ISBN 0-385-48451-8
Grades 9-12

This book records the last course that professor Morrie Schwartz taught the author during his dying days. It is both prosaic and profound. Yes, many of the things that Morrie passed on as his life's learnings were gleaned from others, but that does not detract from their meaningfulness. Nor does it take away from the unique and wonderful way that Morrie strung these gleanings together into a philosophy of life. Everyone who reads this book will be deeply touched.

Main Ideas

 We should live each day as though it were our last.

 Money is not what is important. Love and making a difference in the world are.

 Read the book to find out the other main ideas — it's worth it and Morrie makes these ideas clear in a succinct fashion.

Discussion Starters

- Dying enabled Morrie to focus on those things he considered truly meaningful. List some of these things and comment as to whether or not they are meaningful to you as well, and why.

- On which topic did you find Morrie to be most expert, and what leads you to pick that topic?

- Do you think most people do as much with their last months as Morrie did?

Activities

 Have each student write a paper about an experience he/she had with death. Then, as a class, discuss what, if anything, positive occurred during the time of the loss and afterward as they learned to live with the loss. Share the papers with the class (with permission of all authors, of course).

 If interested in extra reading on this topic, read Elizabeth Kubler-Ross's landmark book *On Death and Dying* (Econo-Clad books, 1999).

 As a class, watch the made-for-television movie of this book either before or after reading it, and then debrief. Ask each student to pick one thing to do, or appreciate, or change, that very day in honor of Morrie. (To obtain the movie, go to www.ABC.com on the Internet. It was broadcast the first week of December, 1999.)

For Further Reading

K-3

Andrews's Angry Words by Dorothea Lachner, illustrated by The Tjong-Khing. North South Books, 1995. 32 pages. ISBN 1-55858-435-8.

    This is a cautionary tale about using angry words, and what can happen when you do. Andrew is angry and he yells at his sister. His bad words keep getting passed from angry person to angry person until they reach a woman who reverses the action and returns angry words with a bundle of kind ones.

Babushka Baba Yaga written and illustrated by Patricia Polacco. Philomel Books, 1993. 32 pages. ISBN 0-399-22531-5.

    What a great book! As it says, "Those who judge one another on what they hear or see, and not on what they know of them in their hearts, are fools indeed!" Polacco's version of this Russian folk tale can be an excellent tool for learning to love each other. As the villagers learned to appreciate Baba Yaga for the wonderful creature she was and not the fearsome one they had heard about, we learn not to judge people on external qualities or supposed characteristics.

The Best of K'tonton by Sadie Rose Weilerstein, illustrated by Marilyn Hirsh. The Jewish Publication Society, 1988. 94 pages. ISBN 0-8276-0187-5.

    K'tonton was created in 1930, and this Jewish "Tom Thumb character" has been in our lives ever since. Nearly all of the 16 stories have ethical lessons to teach. Many of the stories are rooted in the Jewish holidays.

Bone Button Borscht by Aubrey Davis, illustrated by Dušan Petričić. Kids Can Press Ltd., 1997. 32 pages. ISBN 1-55074-224-8.

    This is a very cute retelling of "Stone Soup" set against the background of a Jewish *shtetl* in the Europe of many of our grandparents and great grandparents. The mean and stingy townspeople learn the valuable lesson of sharing from the poor beggar who comes into their town.

Chicken Sunday written and illustrated by Patricia Polacco. Philomel Books, 1992. 32 pages. ISBN 0-399-22133-6.

    This is a lovely, heartwarming story of children who are trying to do a good deed, are misunderstood in the process, clear up the misunderstanding, and accomplish their task as well. It is an excellent example of learning to work out problems with others in our multicultural world, and of the importance of doing good deeds and the ripple effect of performing them.

My Rotten Redheaded Older Brother written and illustrated by Patricia Polacco. Simon & Schuster Books for Young Readers, 1994. 32 pages. ISBN 0-671-72751-6.
> As usual, Ms. Polacco has written a charming and beautiful book, this time about sibling rivalry and getting what you wish for. This autobiographical account of her childhood relationship with her older brother highlights the need for every child to feel that he or she is the best at something. The surprise in this book is finding out what Patricia ends up being better at than her brother Richard, and how that irrevocably changes their relationship for the better.

Yettele's Feathers written and illustrated by Joan Rothenberg. Hyperion Books for Children, 1995. 32 pages. ISBN 0-7868-1149-8.
> If you are teaching about gossip, refer to this book. (See Featured Books, Chapter 3, "Folklore: From Generation To Generation.")

Grades 4-6

God's Mailbox by Marc Gellman, illustrated by Debbie Tilley. Morrow Junior Books, 1996. 111 pages. ISBN 0-688-13169-7.
> (See For Further Reading, Chapter 1, "Bible: In the Beginning.")

The Hopscotch Tree by Leda Siskind. Turtleback, 1995. 120 pages. ISBN 0-606-07661-1.
> This book deals with the issues of prejudice, self-hate, and fitting in. When ten-year-old Edith Gold moves to a new house and to a new school, she encounters a terrible bully named Zandra. She also finds a unique friend — the Hopscotch Tree, a big tree in the school playground. Reading about Edith's problems and how they are resolved can be helpful to children of this age group who may be dealing with similar issues.

The Koufax Dilemma by Steven Schnur, illustrated by Meryl Treatner. William Morrow and Company, Inc., 1997. 186 pages. ISBN 0-688-14221-4.
> This book explores the dilemma often faced by American Jewish youth living in a society that is not responsive to their holidays. Also explored are the issues of divorce and remarriage in families today.

The Peddler's Gift by Maxine Rose Schur, illustrated by Kimberly Bulcken Root. Dial Books for Young Readers, 1999. 32 pages. ISBN 0-8037-1978-7.
> (See Featured Books, Chapter 5, "Holidays: Let's Celebrate!")

Tell Me a Mitzvah: Little and Big Ways to Repair the World by Danny Siegel, illustrated by Judith Friedman. Kar-Ben Copies, Inc., 1993. 64 pages. ISBN 0-929371-78-X.

This thin book is filled with wonderful stories of ordinary people who have done extraordinary good deeds. Each story ends by giving practical ideas to children who are interested in ways to "make the world a better place," as well as to teachers who want to instill the desire to do so in their pupils. This book can be read aloud or alone.

Grades 6-8

Gideon's People by Carolyn Meyer. Harcourt Brace & Company, 1996. 297 pages. ISBN 0-15-200303-7.

After he was hurt in an accident, a 12-year-old Jewish boy, Isaac Litvak, is nursed back to health by an Amish family. Isaac is acutely aware of the differences in this family's way of life and his own Orthodox milieu. There is trouble between the stern Amish father and his 16-year-old son Gideon. When Isaac is finally reunited with his own people, he describes those who cared for him. His friend Abie says, "Whew . . . and I thought only Jews had troubles." A good book about tolerance and about the freedom to choose.

Sarah with an H by Hadley Irwin. Margaret K. McElderry Books, 1996. 134 pages. ISBN 0-689-80949-2.

This novel deals with anti-Semitism in Midwest America. The book begins when Sarah, a Jewish high school junior, and her parents move to a small town in Iowa. It continues by telling the story of the next year and a half and all the difficulties that the family as a whole faces in being accepted as members of this community. Told through the eyes and thoughts of Marti, a hometown girl, it explores prejudice and belonging, without necessarily resolving any of these difficult issues.

Grades 9-12

The Storyteller's Beads by Jane Kurtz. Harcourt Brace & Company, 1998. 154 pages. ISBN 0-15-201074-2.

This is an engrossing fictional account set during the political strife and famine in Ethiopia during the 1980s. Two girls, one Christian and the other Jewish and blind, struggle to overcome many difficulties, including their prejudices about each other, as they make the dangerous journey out of Ethiopia. This is an eye-opening look at a very different part of the world.

Words That Hurt, Words That Heal by Rabbi Joseph Telushkin. Morrow/Avon 1996. 218 pages. ISBN 0-688-12445-3.

This book is an excellent guide to the practice and reason behind ethical language. Telushkin's carefully thought-out arguments in favor of watching our tongues and our tempers will leave readers nodding their heads in agreement. Many of his examples ring true and are things of which we are all guilty. Our language and the words we choose to speak are so important, yet good thoughts often take a back seat to titillating gossip. This is a book that can benefit all who read it.

Grades 11-12

The Reader by Bernhard Schlink. Pantheon Books, 1995. 218 pages. ISBN 0-375-40826-6.

This highly provocative novel is set against the backdrop of the Holocaust. While there are many sexual scenes that may be offensive to some, there are so many ethical dilemmas posed, resolved, not resolved, and examined that the book is included here in the recommended list. Some of the passages are difficult reading, for their emotional as well as their literary content, but perservering is well worth the effort.

All Ages

The Soul Bird by Michal Senunit, illustrated by Na'ama Golomb. Hyperion, 1999. 42 pages. ISBN 0-7868-6519-9.

This lovely little book is both poetic and profound. It can be read by all ages, as it uses very simple language to convey some very important and deep philosophical messages about the relationship between ourselves and our soul. It can be used as a guidebook to assist us in living our lives more truthfully by being in touch with our inner selves and emotions. It also shows us that we have a choice either to pay attention to our soul bird and benefit, or ignore it and live in ignorance and unhappiness.

Chapter 3

Folklore: From Generation To Generation

The richness of Jewish folklore never ceases to amaze. We have stories of the wealthy and the poor, the learned and the ignorant, and the good and the evil. These are most often universal themes with cultural markers that signal us that we are reading (or hearing) a Jewish story. Our folk tales are populated not only by men and women, but by demons, giants, dybbuks, golems, werewolves, angels, and fallen angels. These stories have the power to open minds and hearts. Most of the books featured in this chapter can be shared with children of all ages.

Featured Books

It Could Always Be Worse (PK)
Something from Nothing (PK)
The Treasure (K-3)
The Two Brothers (K-3)
Yettele's Feathers (K-3)
Raisel's Riddle (2-4)
The Sabbath Lion (2-4)
The Adventures of Hershel of Ostropol (4-6)
Golem (4-6)
Mazel and Shlimazel or the Milk of a Lioness (4-6)
While Standing on One Foot (6-8)
Miriam's Tambourine (9-12)

It Could Always Be Worse: A Yiddish Folktale

Retold and illustrated by Margot Zemach
Farrar, Straus & Giroux, 1990
32 pages
ISBN 0-374-33650-4
PK

This classic Yiddish folk tale can be found in many places, but never so delightfully as in Ms. Zemach's award winning rendition. A poor man complains to his Rabbi that his house is too small. The wise Rabbi has the man bring into the house a few animals at a time, thus making matters progressively worse. After the poor man cannot stand it any longer, the Rabbi advises him to let all of the animals out of the house at once. The family is left with a peaceful, "spacious" place to live.

Main Ideas

- No matter how bad things are, they could always be worse.
- Poor people sometimes live in very crowded homes.
- Be happy with what you have.

Discussion Starters

- How many people live in your house or apartment? How many rooms do you share? What do you think it would be like to live in a smaller place?
- Do you think the Rabbi did a good job teaching the poor, unfortunate man what to do?
- To whom would you go if you needed help with a problem?

Activities

 Read the story as different groups of children act out all the sounds in the man's house. After the animals are taken back out, have everyone put down their heads and pretend to sleep and enjoy the quiet.

 Provide magazines and help children find and tear out pictures of animals. Then give them each a big piece of manila paper and a glue stick and have them make an animal collage.

 Provide a big appliance box with a door and windows already cut out. Let the children decorate it inside and out. Then count how many children can fit into the house, having them enter one at a time.

Something from Nothing

Written and illustrated by Phoebe Gilman
Scholastic Trade, 1993
32 pages
ISBN 0-590-47280-1
PK

Gilman has taken a delightful folk tale of love and ingenuity and has made it into a visual feast. A blanket is given to a small child by his grandfather. Over the years, it wears out and is made into a jacket, which eventually is made into a vest, and so forth. Finally, there is nothing left of the original blanket, except a wonderful story! A twist has been added via the illustrated parallel story of a mouse family which lives below the floorboards. Children love to hear this sweet story over and over again. (Other versions of this story are: *Joseph Had a Little Overcoat* by Simms Taback, Penguin Putnam, Inc., 1999, and *Bit by Bit* by Steve Sanfield, illustrated by Susan Gaber, Philomel Books, 1995.)

Main Ideas

- Members of a family can help each other.
- Stories about things that happen to you are important.
- If you think about it, you can find ways to reuse things.

Discussion Starters

- Do you have a favorite blanket or stuffed animal? What does it look like? feel like? smell like?
- How do you think Joseph felt when he lost the button?
- Have any grown-ups in your life made something special for you? Tell about it.

Activities

 Have a show-and-tell in which the children bring in their favorite blanket or stuffed animal (see first question above). Have them tell about who gave it to them and why they love it.

 Point out the illustrations of the parallel mouse family. Then have the children tell its story. You can do this as a round robin or just have those children who want to make up the story tell it.

 Provide sturdy cardboard, white glue, and plenty of buttons for each child to make a button collage. Then have each child dictate a sentence about the artwork to you. Write their sentence along the bottom of their boards.

The Treasure

Written and illustrated by Uri Shulevitz
Farrar, Straus and Giroux, 1979
32 pages
ISBN 0-374-37740-5
K-3

This award winning book has been in print since 1978. It is a story that is told in many cultures, but this is a distinctly Eastern European version. A poor man dreams of finding a treasure. He follows his dream to a distant city only to learn that the real treasure has been in his own home, under his own nose, the whole time. (For older children, you can read "The Dream and the Treasure" in Peninnah Schram's *Jewish Stories One Generation Tells Another*, Jason Aronson Inc., 1987.)

Main Ideas

- Sometimes one must travel far to discover what is near.
- We have treasures in our own homes.
- Dreams are worth following.

Discussion Starters

- What is the meaning of the saying, "Sometimes one must travel far to discover what is near"?
- What kind of treasures do you have in your own home?
- Do you think dreams can give us important messages?

Activities

 Make treasure boxes using cigar or shoe boxes. Have the children decorate them with gold paint and sequins and glitter. Then have the children put photos of their family, friends, and pets inside their boxes.

 Have the children write a story about the guard and what happens when he receives the priceless ruby. Younger children can dictate their stories and accompany them with a drawing.

 Play "I went on a trip and I took . . . " As the group leader, start by saying, "I went on a trip to_____and I took_____with me." Then the next person in the circle repeats what you said and adds another item, and so forth. This is a good memory and listening exercise.

The Two Brothers: A Legend of Jerusalem

Retold and illustrated by Neil Waldman
Atheneum Books for Young Readers, 1997
40 pages
ISBN 0-689-31936-3
K-3

This story has been told for many years as part of the oral tradition. It answers the question, "Why was the Holy Temple built where it was?" Legend has it that in King Solomon's time, two brothers showed how much they cared for each other on a hilltop, and it is from this that Waldman weaves his story of love and miracles. The playful illustrations give a light note to this powerful story.

Main Ideas

- Love between siblings can be powerful.

- Charity can be given selflessly and anonymously.

- God is pleased by acts of loving-kindness.

Discussion Starters

- Do you think it is important that the Holy Temple was built on a place where loving-kindness had been shown? Where else might it have been built?

- Our homes are like little sanctuaries. How do you help to make yours a peaceful and loving place?

- Have you ever done a secret good deed for someone? What was it? Did you get to see the person's reaction? Describe it.

Activities

 Put all the names of your group on slips of paper and into a bag. Have each child pull a name and that person becomes her "Secret Sibling." Instruct the children to do secret good deeds for their secret sibling and at the end of a number of sessions have the children reveal who their secret sibling was. Discuss how it felt to have nice things done for you and to do nice things for others.

 Show your group pictures of replicas of the Temple. (See: *If I Forget Thee, O Jerusalem,* written and photographed by Bernard Wolf, Dutton Children's Books, 1998, pp 10-13.) For older children, read Chapters 5 and 6 of I Kings in the Tanach for a description of Solomon's Temple.

 Make a seed mosaic of the hill on which the two brothers lived. Give each child a piece of sturdy cardboard and white glue. Provide a variety of seeds and beans large enough to handle. Have each child spread glue on their piece of cardboard where the seeds will go, then press the seeds into it. Instruct the children to think about texture and color of the mosaic, as well as the form.

Yettele's Feathers

Written and illustrated by Joan Rothenberg
Hyperion Books for Children, 1995
32 pages
ISBN 0-7868-1149-8
K-3

READ ALOUD

The setting for this retelling of a classic folk tale is an Eastern European *shtetl* (a small Jewish town or village). Yettele Babbelonski is a lonely woman who loves to gossip. After passing along many stories, Yettele finds that no one will talk to her. So she turns to the Rabbi. He decides to teach Yettele a lesson, demonstrating that words can be very harmful and cannot be taken back. The colorful gouache illustrations lend a comic note to this moral tale.

Main Ideas

 Words can be harmful.

 Gossip spreads.

 Words cannot be taken back.

Discussion Starters

- Do you think the Rabbi was too hard on Yettele by making her gather up all the feathers? Could she have learned her lesson an easier way?

- What could you do if someone starts to tell you some gossip about someone else?

- If you are lonely, or need help with a problem, to whom can you turn for help?

Activities

 Play a game of telephone. Everyone sits in a circle. The "Yettele" (the one who will start the story) thinks of something to say, then whispers it into the next person's ear. That person tries to repeat it just as it was said into the next person's ear, and so forth. The last person says the message out loud, and "Yettele" reports if what she now hears is what she actually said.

 Fill a cloth bag with small craft feathers before your group convenes. In front of the children, shake the bag out and let the feathers fly. Allow the children to see for themselves how difficult it is to collect the feathers. Then talk again about trying to take back words.

 Yettele is a lonely woman. At the end of the story, she has learned to tell stories about herself rather than about others. Arrange for the children to visit with some elders in your community. Either invite them to your class or plan a visit to a Seniors' Center. Have the children ask about what it was like when the seniors were little (they can prepare specific questions before the visit). Perhaps you can make an audiotape or videotape of the session. And by all means, serve *rugelach* and tea!

Raisel's Riddle

By Erica Silverman
Illustrated by Susan Gaber
Farrar, Straus and Giroux, 1999
40 pages
ISBN 0-374-36168-1
Grades 2-4

Here is the Cinderella story recast in Poland at Purim time and starring a young, educated Jewish girl. Raisel earns her three wishes by giving her own plate of food to a beggar woman. She also captivates the heart of the Rabbi's son with her knowledge, which is demonstrated through a riddle: What is more precious than rubies, more lasting than gold? What can never be traded, stolen, or sold? What comes with great effort and takes time, but then, once yours, will serve you again and again?

Main Ideas

- Knowledge is precious.
- Good deeds may be rewarded.
- How someone behaves is more important than how a person looks.

Discussion Starters

- Raisel tells the Rabbi's son, "Look not at the flask, but at what it contains." What does she mean by this?
- Discuss the "winning" riddle (see above). What does each part of it mean? Is there anything other than learning or knowledge that might work as an answer?
- In what ways are *Raisel's Riddle* and *Cinderella* similar? In what ways are they different?

Activities

 Raisel is rewarded for her kindness to the beggar woman. Hunger is a very prevalent problem in our society. Arrange to collect and donate food to a community food pantry or kitchen, or to help out in a community shelter.

 At the Purim ball, a *klezmer* band is making music. Play some *klezmer* music and have the children play musical chairs. (*Klezmer* is a style of Jewish music prevalent in Eastern Europe.) Children can also try to identify the different instruments.

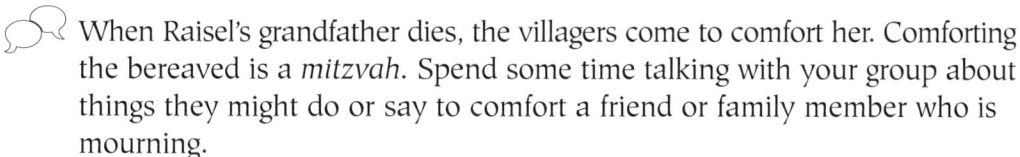 When Raisel's grandfather dies, the villagers come to comfort her. Comforting the bereaved is a *mitzvah*. Spend some time talking with your group about things they might do or say to comfort a friend or family member who is mourning.

The Sabbath Lion: A Jewish Folktale from Algeria

Retold by Howard Schwartz and Barbara Rush
Illustrated by Stephen Fieser
Harper Trophy, 1996
32 pages
ISBN 0-06-44382-X
Grades 2-4

READ ALOUD

Young Yosef is sent with a caravan on a journey across the desert from Algeria to Cairo. Unfortunately, the caravan leader does not keep his promise to stop and rest on the Sabbath. Yosef decides to leave the safety of the caravan rather than break the rules of the day of rest. Miraculously, a magnificent lion appears to spend the Sabbath with Yosef and to accompany him to Cairo and then home.

Main Ideas

- The Sabbath is a sacred day.

- It is important to do what you believe in.

- Miracles do happen.

Discussion Starters

- Yosef helps his family in many ways. What do you do to help your family? What could you do to help your family?

- How does your family celebrate the Sabbath? In what way would you like to celebrate Shabbat?

- How do you think the lion knew to find and help Yosef?

Activities

 Jews live all over the world. Show your group a world map or globe. Point out where they live. Now show them Algeria and Egypt. Give each child a world map to take home. Ask each to find out where their family members came from, then to color in those parts of the world. Have the children bring back the maps. Tack them up on the walls. How many different places are colored in?

 Bring in some spices of the Middle East (e.g., cardamom, cinnamon, mace, nutmeg, allspice, dried pepper, cloves, turmeric, fresh ginger, dried lavender flowers, and rosebuds). Figs, dates, and oranges are fragrant fruits of the region and can also be used. Have the children smell each, then describe the smells and colors. Perhaps you can offer oranges and Fig Newtons for a snack.

 Yosef celebrated the Sabbath in the desert surrounded by sand. Make sand art Sabbath candle holders. Provide two tumblers, two votive candles, and a variety of colored sands for each child. Instruct them to layer the colored sand and set the candles firmly into the centers. Teach the blessing for the Sabbath candles.

The Adventures of Hershel of Ostropol

Retold by Eric A. Kimmel
Illustrated by Trina Schart Hyman
Holiday House, 1995
64 pages
ISBN 0-8234-1210-5
Grades 4-6

READ ALOUD

READ ALONE

READ TOGETHER

This is a collection of ten stories about the folk hero Hershel of Ostropol. Kimmel claims Hershel was a real person who lived in the first part of the nineteenth century in the Ukraine. Herschel was a trickster of the first order, living by his wits and good fortune. The people of the towns he visited saw their lives in his, and have passed down his stories and jests, making Hershel immortal. Let's share his stories and sayings with our children, lest they be forgotten.

Main Ideas

- The tales of Hershel transmit values and cultural traditions of Eastern European Jewry.

- The trickster character in folklore can think of all kinds of ways to get out of a jam.

- Jewish folklore is filled with proverbs.

Discussion Starters

- Which is your favorite story in this collection, and why?

- In the story "The Candlesticks," it is said: " . . . a good deed is a good deed, even when it is done unwillingly." In this story, Hershel's Uncle Zalman gives charity unknowingly. Do you think this still counts as a good deed? Defend your position.

Is there anyone in your family who reminds you of Hershel — someone who is a good storyteller or who is always saying proverbs? Tell a story about that person.

Activities

 In the story "The Miracle," Rabbi Israel refers to two prophets, Elijah (I Kings 17) and Elisha (II Kings 4), who were able to revive the dead. Study these two passages with your class.

 In an "Incredible Story," Hershel tells a nonsense story. Have a storytelling contest. Whoever tells the most ridiculous story wins!

 At the end of the book, there is a list of "Hershel's Sayings." Write these on strips of paper and have groups of two or three pick one out of a bag and make up a little story or draw a picture to illustrate it.

Golem

Written and illustrated by David Wisniewski
Clarion Books, 1996
32 pages
ISBN 0-395-72618-2
Grades 4-6

READ ALOUD

Although this is a picture book (Caldecott Medal, 1997), it is not a book for very young children. Set in sixteenth century Prague, *Golem* is the eternal story of the persecuted who call upon the supernatural for protection. This legend is retold here with pathos, sweeping drama, and masterly cut-paper illustrations. It is a thought provoking look at power, prejudice, and justice. An endnote provides historical references. (See also *The Golem* by Barbara Rogasky, illustrated by Trina Schart Hyman, Holiday House, 1996, and *The Golem* by I.B. Singer, illustrated by Uri Shulevitz, Sunburst, 1996.)

Main Ideas

- According to legend, Rabbi Judah Loew ben Bezalel of Prague created a Golem to protect the Jews.

- The Blood Lie, or Blood Libel, was slander that caused great harm to Jews.

- Human power is limited.

Discussion Questions

- Why did Rabbi Loew write the word *emet* (truth) on the Golem's forehead?

- The Golem asks whether it was wise for him to be created. What do you think he meant?

- Do you think the excessive force and destruction the Golem used against those attacking the ghetto was justified?

Activities

 Prague, now in the Czech Republic, is a wonderful city to visit. Try to find someone in your community who has traveled there to share their impressions, photographs, and stories with your group.

The art of paper cutting is a traditional one among many people, including the Jews. Have your group create one (or more) rectangular shaped cut-paper *mizrach,* to be placed on the eastern wall of your meeting room or in the children's homes. Such a *mizrach* indicates the direction to face when praying. It should have the word מִזְרָח (*mizrach*, meaning East) on it. Make these on white paper mounted on dark. The cut designs can be lightly tinted with watercolor. Provide scissors designed for fine cutting, as well as some samples of Jewish motifs that can be used. It will take several tries at design and cutting to be successful. (For more information on how to do paper cutting, consult *The Second Jewish Catalog* by Sharon Strassfeld and Michael Strassfeld, Jewish Publication Society, 1976, pp. 324-326.)

Have your group discuss what threats exist today for Jews and whether a Golem would help. If so, what would a modern Golem look like, and how would it behave? Have individuals or the class as a whole write modern day Golem stories using these ideas.

Mazel and Schlimazel or the Milk of the Lioness

By Isaac Bashevis Singer
Translated by Elizabeth Shub
Photographs by Margot Zemach
Turtleback, 1995
48 pages
ISBN 0-606-09602-7
Grades 4-6

Nobel Prize winner I.B. Singer took a traditional folktale and made it into a classic story that can be enjoyed by all ages. Margot Zemach has added her vigorous drawings to enliven this contest between good luck and bad luck and the saga of their unwitting guinea pig, a young man named Tam.

Main Ideas

- Perhaps good luck is really a result of good behavior.

- Good luck and bad luck play roles in peoples' lives.

- The use of a wrong word can get you into trouble.

Discussion Starters

- Why did Mazel call the wine of forgetfulness precious? What kinds of things are good to forget? What kinds of things do you want to remember forever?

- What did Princess Nesika mean when she said, "If the head is foolish, the feet are foolish"?

- Tam learns that good luck follows those who are diligent, honest, sincere, and helpful to others. What do you think it means to be lucky?

Activities

 Tam is given the Order of Selfless Devotion. Have your group come up with other medals that might be awarded to people who lead good lives. Now have them design and make these medals. Provide sturdy cardboard, scissors, a hole puncher, 3-D (puffy) paints, sequins, glue, and ribbons. Orchestrate an awards ceremony.

 Have the class compose a list of all the lucky and unlucky things that have happened to them. Lead the discussion so that for each unlucky thing, they may be able to think of a lucky thing that came of it.

Read more stories by Isaac Bashevis Singer. The collection *Stories for Children* (see For Further Reading at the end of this chapter) has 35 others from which to choose.

While Standing on One Foot: Puzzle Stories and Wisdom Tales from the Jewish Tradition

By Nina Jaffe and Steve Zeitlin
Illustrated by John Segal
Henry Holt, 1996
128 pages
ISBN 0-8050-5073-6
Grades 6-8

READ ALOUD

READ ALONE

READ TOGETHER

In this valuable collection, 18 stories from around the world have been transferred to different periods of Jewish history. Each story begins with a short, informative introduction. Before it ends, the authors pose a question, challenging the readers to think about possible endings. Each story provides topics which will lead to plenty of discussion.

Main Ideas

- Stories can pose and answer many kinds of questions.
- The Jewish tradition tells of many people who have survived by their wits.
- Jewish stories come from a multitude of sources.

Discussion Starters

- Which is your favorite story in this collection? Were you able to guess its ending?
- What lessons do the stories in this volume teach?

In the epilogue, the authors use a story to illustrate that wisdom is handed down in stories. Have your parents or grandparents told you stories in order to pass down wisdom? What stories? Which of the stories will you tell to your children, and why?

Activities

 Have each child choose a favorite story from the book. Then direct each to the source notes at the end of the book. Send students to the library, to the Internet, and to their families to see how many versions of the story they can find.

 Play a game of "physical telephone." Have the group stand in a circle and one person performs a movement (with or without an accompanying sound). The next person repeats that movement exactly as they believe they saw it. No corrections from leader or other participants. The following person in turn mimics the movement from the second person (not the originator), and so forth around the circle. By the time the movement is done by the last student, chances are it will have changed. Explain that just as the original movement changed as it passed to different people, stories change in the oral tradition.

 Have each child tell their favorite story. They can tell it just as it is in the book (though it should not be memorized but paraphrased), or another version that they find in their research, or one that they create by combining different versions. Some students might want to take the story and reset it in time and place. Anything is possible, as long as the student remembers to credit his/her sources and stay true to the original message in the story.

Miriam's Tambourine: Jewish Folktales from around the World

Selected and retold by Howard Schwartz
Illustrated by Lloyd Bloom
Oxford University Press, 1988
393 pages
ISBN 0-19-282136-9
Grades 9-12

READ ALOUD

READ ALONE

READ TOGETHER

The 50 tales contained in this book are drawn from different regions of the world. They reflect different periods of time and the diversity of Jewish history. These stories go far beyond the better known stories of poor beggars and wise Rabbis. The collection includes demons, enchanted palaces, the terror of the pogroms, and the longing of Jews to return to the Land of Israel. As always, Howard Schwartz has meticulously annotated his sources.

Main Ideas

- The aspects of a Jewish folktale are: Jewish time, Jewish place, Jewish characters, Jewish message.

- Many Jewish stories can be recognized as variants of familiar secular stories.

- Stories can be read on many levels.

Discussion Starters

- Which of these is your favorite story, and how does it apply to your life?

- What makes a folktale Jewish?

- Other than folktales, what other kinds of stories do we have in the Jewish tradition?

Activities

 Have each student pick a story to work with, then do the following:

Decide the most important thing about the story and write it down in one sentence. (Storyteller Doug Lipman calls this the MIT — "most important thing.")

Using the story at least in part, write a sermon that addresses the MIT.

 Research the sources of a story in this collection and give an oral report on the region from which the story comes, its period in history, its variants (other versions of the story), and its Jewish markers (that which makes it Jewish, i.e., time, place, character, message).

 Choose a story in the book and make a pictorial story board of it. Lay out paper marked in squares like a comic strip. Draw pictures in each square representing the sequence of the story. Students can generate computer art or use collage materials if they prefer.

For Further Reading

K-3

Bone Button Borscht by Aubrey Davis, illustrated by Dušan Petričić. Kids Can Press Ltd., 1997. 32 pages. ISBN 1-55074-224-8.
   (See For Further Reading, Chapter 2: "Ethics: Doing the Right Thing.")

Dybbuk: A Story Made in Heaven by Francine Prose, illustrated by Mark Podwal. Greenwillow Books, 1996. 24 pages. ISBN 0-688-14307-5.
   In this beautifully illustrated book, Prose has combined the legend of the angels making matches in heaven before babies are born with a sneezing *dybbuk* (a spirit with unfinished business who enters the body of an innocent person). She has created a story filled with magic and laughter.

Just Stay Put by Gary Clement. Groundwood Books, 1996. 32 pages. ISBN 0-88899-239-4.
   After some background on the people of Chelm, the author tells of Mendel, a daydreamer, who dreams of going to Warsaw. While on his journey, Mendel carefully points his shoes in the direction of Warsaw when he decides to take a nap. A thief comes along and turns the shoes around, pointing them toward Chelm. Imagine foolish Mendel's surprise when Warsaw is exactly like Chelm! He reasons that "if one place is exactly like every other place, one might as well just stay put."

Onions and Garlic: An Old Tale by Eric Kimmel, illustrated by Katya Arnold. Holiday House, 1996. 32 pages. ISBN 0-8234-1222-9.
   This story makes use of a universal folk theme: the kind but foolish brother who brings home a fortune (in this case he trades onions for diamonds) and his greedy brother who tries to follow suit, but comes back no better off than when he started out (trading garlic for onions). This book could lead to a discussion about what is *really* valuable. The humorous text is accompanied by energetic and playful illustrations.

The Sign in Mendel's Window by Mildred Phillips, illustrated by Margot Zemach. Aladdin Paperbacks, 1996 (reissue). 32 pages. ISBN 0-689-80979-4.
   When a conniving man named Mr. Tinker rents half of Mendel the butcher's shop, trouble is not far behind. Mr. Tinker tries to frame Mendel for theft, but the butcher's clever wife Molly proves that the stranger is the real thief.

The Way Meat Loves Salt: A Cinderella Tale from the Jewish Tradition by Nina Jaffe, illustrated by Louise August. Henry Holt and Company, 1998. 32 pages. ISBN 0-8050-4384-5.

> This Yiddish folk tale is a delightful mixture of Cinderella and King Lear. A Rabbi asks his daughters how much they love him. When he does not understand his youngest daughter's answer ("the way meat likes salt"), he banishes her. The prophet Elijah leads her to another home and gives her a magic stick that makes her wishes come true. The rest is very much like the familiar Cinderella story and leads to a lesson about loving-kindness.

You Never Know: A Legend of the Lamed-vavniks by Francine Prose, illustrated by Mark Podwal. Greenwillow Books, 1998. 24 pages. ISBN 0-688-15806-4.

> This is an updated version of the legend of the *lamed-vavniks*, or the 36 righteous people who are secretly on earth at any given time. It is simply and beautifully retold by Ms. Prose, and Mr. Podwal's art is luminous as always.

Grades 4-8

The Diamond Tree: Jewish Tales from around the World retold by Howard Schwartz and Barbara Rush, illustrated by Uri Shulevitz. HarperCollins Publishers, 1998 (reprint). 112 pages. ISBN 0-06-440695-4.

> This is a collection of 15 stories that are drawn from a variety of Jewish sources and parts of the world. There are stories about the giant Og, Noah's helper, a bear who ate children and the mother who saved them, and many other kinds of whimsical delights. Each story teaches a lesson and reflects the region from which it comes.

Next Year in Jerusalem: 3000 Years of Jewish Stories retold by Howard Schwartz, illustrated by Neil Waldman. Puffin, 1999 (reprint). 64 pages. ISBN 0-14-037559-7.

> Folklorist Howard Schwartz has gathered 11 stories from nearly as many countries to portray Jerusalem. In this book, he has combined folklore, Midrash, and legend. An introduction and sidebars throughout the book give historical information, while the stories themselves invite the imagination to soar.

Rachel the Clever and Other Jewish Folktales selected and retold by Josepha Sherman. August House Publishers, 1993. 172 pages. ISBN 0-87483-307-8.

> Sherman retells some very well-known tales in simple language that is ideal for storytelling. The stories come from Europe, North Africa, the Middle East, central Asia, and a few from the Talmud. Magic, wisdom, and mystical beings are presented, along with some short tales from those wise men of Chelm.

The Wise Men of Helm and Their Merry Tales by Solomon Simon, illustrated by Lillian Fischel. Behrman House, 1996 (reissue). 136 pages. ISBN 0-87441-469-5.

This charming collection was originally published in Yiddish in 1942, and it continues to tickle the funny bone. As Mr. Simon says, "Some people say that the wise men of Helm are fools. Don't you believe it. It's just that foolish things are always happening to them."

Grades 9-12

Elijah's Violin and Other Jewish Fairy Tales selected and retold by Howard Schwartz, illustrated by Linda Heller. Oxford University Press, 1994 (reprint). 308 pages. ISBN 0-19-509200-7.

Gabriel's Palace: Jewish Mystical Tales selected and retold by Howard Schwartz. Oxford University Press, 1994 (reprint). 414 pages. ISBN 0-19-509388-7.

Lilith's Cave: Jewish Tales of the Supernatural selected and retold by Howard Schwartz. Oxford University Press, 1991 (reprint). 274 pages. ISBN 0-19-506726-6.

Put the above three volumes on your bookshelf, along with *Miriam's Tambourine,* and you will have a story for any occasion or mood. Schwartz has collected these Jewish tales and has presented them with spellbinding skill. Every story has notes as to its origins, variants, and meanings.

The Jewish Spirit: A Celebration in Stories and Art edited by Ellen Frankel. Stewart, Tabori & Chang, 1997. 240 pages. ISBN 1-55670-623-5.

Imagine opening a book and being greeted by the artistic offerings of Mark Podwal, Ben Shahn, and Marc Chagall. Then combine their magnificent art with the stories of Rabbi Nachman of Bratzlav, Sholom Aleichem, Francine Prose, I.L. Peretz, and with folktales from exotic lands, and you've got a book to cherish. The section headings are: "Beginnings," "Coming of Age," "Family," "Marriage," "Community," "In the Heart of Wisdom," and "The End of Days." The stories are fuel for endless conversation and the pictures are worth thousands of words.

All Ages

Angels, Prophets, Rabbis & Kings from the Stories of the Jewish People by José Patterson, illustrated by Claire Bushe and Edward Ripley. Peter Bedrick Books, 1991. 144 pages. ISBN 0-87226-912-4.

This handsome book combines stories from the Bible, Talmud, and folklore. The author begins with a Midrash about creation and the letters of the alphabet. He concludes with a moving folktale, "Bontshe the Silent," about the request of an exceedingly humble man when he arrives in heaven. It is an excellent companion book when studying about the Jewish people.

Jewish Stories One Generation Tells Another by Peninnah Schram. Jason Aronson Inc., 1996. 508 pages. ISBN 1-56821-980-6.

In this collection, master storyteller Peninnah Schram has gently reframed some of our most beloved stories. She introduces each story with notes and explanations which are helpful to anyone who wishes to research the tales further. This is a useful resource for any classroom or home.

Journeys with Elijah: Eight Tales of the Prophet by Barbara Diamond Goldin, paintings by Jerry Pinkney. Gulliver Books, 1999. 96 pages. ISBN 0-15-200445-9.

The Mysterious Visitor: Stories of the Prophet Elijah by Nina Jaffe, illustrated by Elivia Savadier. Scholastic Press, 1997. 112 pages. ISBN 0-590-48422-2.

Tales of Elijah the Prophet by Peninnah Schram. Jason Aronson, 1997. 312 pages. ISBN 0-7657-5991-8.

The above three collections tell stories of the beloved prophet Elijah. While he is a forbidding character in the Bible, folklore has transformed Elijah into a compassionate champion of the poor and humble. These authors have drawn on many sources to create these lovely books.

Stories for Children by Isaac Bashevis Singer. Sunburst, 1991 (reissue). 352 pages. ISBN 0-374-46489-8.

This superb volume contains 36 stories by the Nobel Prize winner, including some of his most famous, such as "Zlateh the Goat," "Mazel and Shlimazel," and "The Fools of Chelm and the Stupid Carp." These stories are as much fun for adults to read to themselves as they are to read out loud to anyone who will listen. Singer's respect for the written word shines throughout.

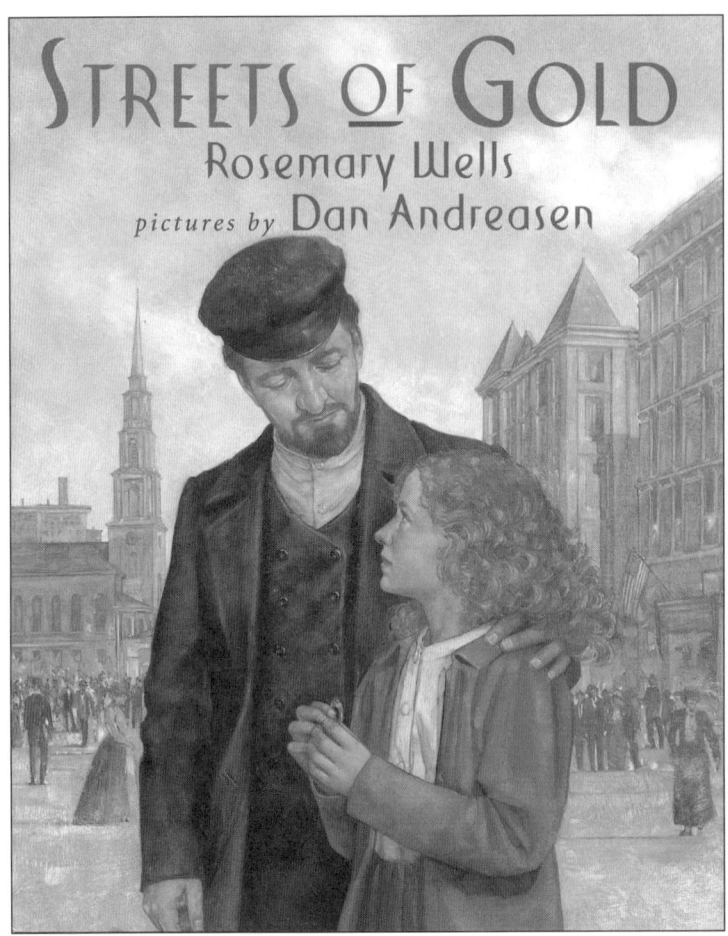

Chapter 4

History: 4,000 Years and Counting

The philosopher George Santayana said that "those who cannot remember the past are condemned to repeat it." Sometimes it seems as if the Jewish people have been condemned to repeat the past regardless of whether we chose to remember it or not. The history of the Jews is filled with persecution, oppression, discrimination, mass genocide, and dislocation. It is astonishing that such a small group of people has elicited such hatred and prejudice. It is equally astonishing to learn about the heroism of so many of our ancestors and their constant striving for the right to live peacefully as Jews. It is only now, with the freedoms provided in democratic countries, that we are finally able to pursue our lives in relative peace and safety. The books in this chapter reflect both the difficulties and the heroism that characterize Jewish history.

Featured Books

The Castle on Hester Street (PK)
The Secret Grove (K-3)
Streets of Gold (K-3)
Molly's Pilgrim (2-4)
Call Me Ruth (4-6)
The Golden City (4-6)
Strudel Stories (4-6)
The Circlemaker (6-8)
Letters from Rifka (6-8)
A Time of Angels (6-8)
The Cure (9-12)
Masada (9-12)

The Castle on Hester Street

Written and illustrated by Linda Heller
The Jewish Publication Society, 1984
32 pages
ISBN 0-8276-0206-5
PK

This is a charming reconstruction of Julie's grandparents' past and how they came to America as young adult immigrants. The story is wonderful, warm, witty, and wacky. Grandpa Sol has a personality that leaps right off the page and will delight small children.

Main Ideas

- A long time ago, life was hard for Jews in other countries.

- There are always at least two ways to look at the past.

- Grandparents often have interesting stories — whether they are real or made up!

Discussion Starters

- Is life hard for Jews now in your country?

- Whose stories did you like better, Grandpa Sol's or Grandma Rose's, and why?

- Which picture did you like the best, and why?

Activities

 Draw a big castle and have the children illustrate the rooms with pictures they think tell this story. Hang the pictures, then reread the story and see if children think the pictures are accurate. If not, fix them!

 Collect clothing buttons. Have the children bring them in regularly. Then, as a class make a mural/collage using the buttons. Donate the piece of artwork to a local nursing home.

 Have each child ask their grandma, grandpa, or any older person they know, to write down one story about their youth that could be shared with the class. It would be a good idea if the older person would come to class and share his/her story in person. You might also ask him/her to speak about the most important Jewish event in his/her life.

The Secret Grove

By Barbara Cohen
Illustrated by Michael J. Deraney
UAHC Press, 1985
32 pages
ISBN 0-8074-0301-6
K-3

This is a story of two young boys in Israel, one Jewish and one Jordanian, who meet two times in an orange grove between their border villages. It explores prejudice, nationalism, the Israeli/Arab conflict, stereotyping, and friendship, while also raising provocative questions.

Main Ideas

- The relationships between Arabs and Israelis are difficult.
- Friendship means learning about other people.
- Sometimes we think we know about other people before we meet them.

Discussion Starters

- How did you feel when the Jewish children said what they said about Arab children?
- How did you feel when Ahmed showed Beni the picture in his history book?
- Could Ahmed and Beni have done anything differently so that their relationship could continue? What about as adults?

Activities

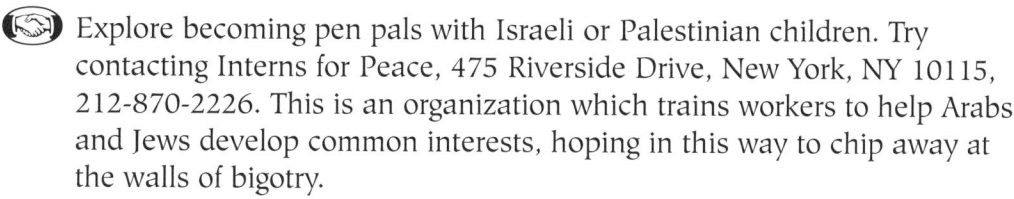 Explore becoming pen pals with Israeli or Palestinian children. Try contacting Interns for Peace, 475 Riverside Drive, New York, NY 10115, 212-870-2226. This is an organization which trains workers to help Arabs and Jews develop common interests, hoping in this way to chip away at the walls of bigotry.

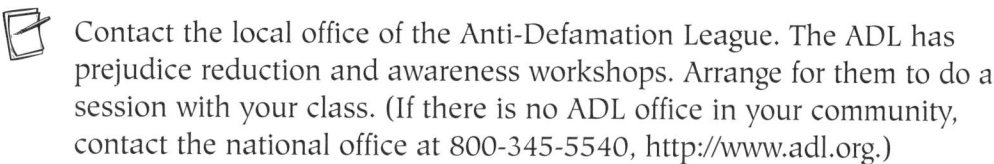 Contact the local office of the Anti-Defamation League. The ADL has prejudice reduction and awareness workshops. Arrange for them to do a session with your class. (If there is no ADL office in your community, contact the national office at 800-345-5540, http://www.adl.org.)

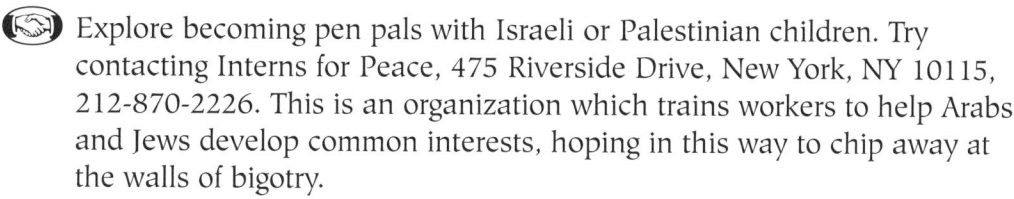 Help students brainstorm something they could do to reduce prejudice (letter to the editor, meeting/helping children from other backgrounds, etc.). Then do one or more of these things as a class.

Streets of Gold

By Rosemary Wells
Illustrated by Dan Andreasen
Dial Books for Young Readers, 1999
40 pages
ISBN 0-8037-2149-8
K-3

This is a child's version of a book the author found on a back shelf of her local library — *The Promised Land* by Mary Antin. It is the story of a young Jewish girl living in the 1890s in Czarist Russia and how she came to emigrate to America. Its excellent illustrations, quotes from Mary herself on each page, and the map of her voyage are all effective additions to the story.

Main Ideas

- Many Russian Jews came to America in late 1800s.
- Girls weren't able to go to school in the past.
- Families often work together to get something done.

Discussion Starters

- Compare Czar Alexander to George Washington — what made one a better leader?
- Why was the story of Blind David included in this book? Was it Blind David who gave Mary's father the sapphire ring?
- Do you agree with Mary "that you had to be an American to understand these mysteries" that made up her American experience?

Activities

 In the book, find the poem by Mary Antin from the *Boston Herald* and have the class read it. Then, have them write their own poem about George Washington or America.

 Explore the Russian Jewish experience. Find out if any student has a relative that has memories of or memorabilia from Russia. Invite that person to class. Or, try cooking/eating Russian Jewish foods (blintzes, borscht, babka cake, etc.).

 Show selected portions of the video *Fiddler on the Roof* so children can see what life was like in Russia during this time. To extend this activity, obtain the CD or audiotape of the show. Have the class pick and learn their favorite songs, then invite families to a performance.

Molly's Pilgrim

By Barbara Cohen
Illustrated by Daniel Mark Duffy
Lothrop Lee and Shepard, 1998 (revised edition)
32 pages
ISBN 0-688-16279-7
Grades 2-4

This revised edition is the story of a young girl, Molly, who is told to make a Pilgrim doll for a Thanksgiving display at school. Molly is ashamed when her mother tries to help by creating a doll dressed as she herself was dressed before leaving Russia to seek religious freedom in America. Molly's teacher handles Molly's embarrassment wisely, and guides her class toward renewed tolerance. Barbara Cohen's classic inspired an Academy Award winning short film.

Main Ideas

- There has been a promise of religious freedom in America since the days of the original Pilgrims.
- The American holiday of Thanksgiving is based on Sukkot.
- The immigrant experience in America extends beyond New York City.

Discussion Starters

- How are the original Pilgrims to America like the immigrants of later times?
- How is Thanksgiving like Sukkot? How is it different?
- Molly's mother speaks Yiddish. Do you know where Yiddish originated? Do you know any words in Yiddish?

Activities

 Invite recent Jewish immigrants to your classroom. Have the children ask questions about the life they left "on the other side" and about what is different about living in America. Have your guests talk about the difficulty of learning a new language. Have them teach your students some words in their native tongue. End the session with a feast of "Thanksgiving."

 Teach some Yiddish. Molly's mother uses the following expressions: *shaynkeit* (beauty), *oi, Malkeleh* (Oh, Molly), *nu, Malkeleh* (what then, Molly), *nu, shaynkeit* (so, my beautiful one), *mazel tov* (good luck), *Bubbe* (Grandmother), *Zayde* (Grandfather). Have your children ask their parents and grandparents, aunts, and uncles for more Yiddish words to bring in to share with the class.

 View the video *Molly's Pilgrim* and compare it to the book. This outstanding dramatic presentation is intermixed with humor, and teaches valuable lessons about tolerance and *kavod ha-briot* (respect for all God's creatures). The video can be rented from the Board of Jewish Education of Greater New York, 212-586-8200, ext. 316.

Call Me Ruth

By Marilyn Sachs
Beech Tree Books, 1995 (reprint)
134 pages
ISBN 0-688-13737-7
Grades 4-6

Set at the turn of the twentieth century, *Call Me Ruth* is an engaging narrative of the Jewish immigrant experience. The story takes place in New York City during the Labor Movement's early struggles. The novel clearly and painfully describes from a young girl's point of view the tensions between two generations of new arrivals.

Main Ideas

- There was considerable oppression of the Jews in Eastern Europe in the late nineteenth and early twentieth centuries.

- Many people immigrated to New York City at the beginning of the twentieth century.

- Jewish women played a major role in the Labor Movement.

Discussion Starters

- Ruth's cousin Shirley says, "Everyone is the same here." Do you think everyone is the same in your country?

- Through most of this book, Ruth feels ashamed of her mother. Have you ever felt ashamed about a parent or other grown-up relative? Describe the situation and why you were ashamed. What did you do about your feelings?

Many of the characters in this book are very concerned with how they and others are dressed. What do you think clothing can tell about a person? (See the first activity below.)

Activities

 Assign roles and read aloud the folk tale: "Welcome to Clothes" from Peninnah Schram's *Tales of Elijah* the Prophet, Jason Aronson Inc., 1991, or *The Wise Shoemaker of Studena* by Syd Lieberman, The Jewish Publication Society, 1994. You can collect clothing to donate and have a day when the kids dress without any fashion labels showing.

 Using a current world map and one with 1909 borders, trace the journey to America of Ruth and her mother. Draw the route on a piece of paper, make several copies, cut the routes up and have teams put them back together.

 Research the role Jews played in the Shirtwaist Makers Strike of 1909. Write for information to UNITE! The Union of Needle trades, Industrial and Textile Employees, 1710 Broadway, New York, NY 10019, or visit their Web page at www.uniteunion.org.

The Golden City: Jerusalem's 3,000 Years

Written and Illustrated by Neil Waldman
Boyds Mills Press, 2000
32 pages
ISBN 1-56397-918-7
Grades 4-6

READ ALONE

This beautifully illustrated book tells the history of Jerusalem's 3,000 years. The history of this beautiful city parallels the history of the Jewish people, especially as so much of the story of the Jews took place there. There is an excellent time line at the end of the book.

Main Ideas

 Jerusalem is the focal point for three major religions.

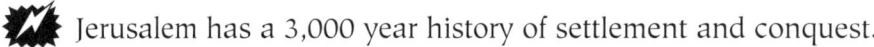 Jerusalem has a 3,000 year history of settlement and conquest.

 Jerusalem is important to Jews and to the modern state of Israel.

Discussion Starters

- What do you think was the most important event that occurred in Jerusalem? Explain your answer.

- Have you ever been to Jerusalem? What were your impressions?

- Why do we end our Pesach *Seder* every year by saying, *"LaShanah Haba'ah B'Yerushalyim"* (Next year in Jerusalem)?

Activities

 This book can be paired with *The Two Brothers: A Legend of Jerusalem* (Chapter 4, "Folklore: From Generation To Generation"), thereby giving the legend behind the city. Have children read both and then discuss ways that the legend is different from actual history.

 Illustrate the time line at the end of the book in one of the following ways: (1) each child gets one date from the time line to illustrate and when all the illustrations are done, put them together; or (2) as a group, write out the time line on a long piece of craft paper and draw illustrations above or below each date.

 Put up photographs of Jerusalem around the room. Ask questions about Jerusalem that teams must answer cooperatively to move from photo to photo. The first team to get to the Western Wall wins. (If you wish, you can have students do a physical task to earn their Jerusalem question to make the game last longer — e.g., everyone on the team must do 30 sit-ups, 50 jumping jacks, hop on one foot for 30 seconds.)

Strudel Stories

By Joanne Rocklin
Yearling Books, 2000
131 pages
ISBN 0-440-41509-8
Grades 4-6

This warm and touching novel follows a Jewish family through seven generations and more than 100 years as they brave war, dare the difficulties of immigration, and enjoy the simple pleasures of family, friendship, sports, and making strudel. The family stories are "folded into" the strudels, generation to generation. This book should definitely be read with adult guidance, as it is a serious introduction to death and the Holocaust.

Main Ideas

- Families often have traditions that are very interesting and worth preserving.
- Traditions are a way of keeping our ancestors alive inside of us.
- There was significant Jewish immigration from Russia to America in the late 1800s and from Hungary after World War II.

Discussion Starters

- Which was your favorite story and storyteller? Explain your answer.
- When have you ever completely transformed your view of another person, as Willy did of Leon?
- Who do you think was the bravest character, and what were his/her actions that lead you to that conclusion?

Activities

 The most obvious activity — and one that will be a lot of fun — is to make one of the strudel recipes in the book. The most practical of these will probably be the shortcut strudel, as the others take much longer (or are in Yiddish, which might make it difficult to figure out).

 Have each child interview his or her parents to find out from which countries his/her ancestors came, then help each to cut out the shape of each of the countries. Use these shapes to make a "country collage." Post it on the class bulletin board.

 Ask students about their family's traditions. Perhaps each week, a student could bring in (as if for show-and-tell) a tradition that is particular to their family. If they cannot discover one, perhaps they, with other family members, can institute a new family tradition and then share it with the class.

The Circlemaker

By Maxine Rose Schur
Econo-Clad Books, 1999
182 pages
ISBN 0-7857-9240-6
Grades 6-8

This engrossing novel portrays life in Russia for Jews under the rule of Czar Nicholas I in the early and mid 1800s. This cruel Czar made a law in 1827 that Jewish boys from age 12 to 18 were to be conscripted into the army. They received military and religious (Christian) instruction until they were 18, then began their 25-year service. More than 50,000 Jewish boys were taken during the 30 years of this law. Most were forcibly converted, and nearly half did not survive their experiences. In this book, we meet Mendel, a 12-year-old Jewish boy, who lives in the Ukraine with his parents in Molovsk, a small village. When the Czar's soldiers come riding into their village in April of 1852 to take all eligible Jewish youth for the army, he runs away and tries to get to his aunt in America. His story will keep the readers' interest as they learn about this period of Jewish history.

Main Ideas

- Jews were often at the mercy of tyrannical leaders who made horrible laws.
- Freedom is a goal worth pursuing.
- We all have a place in the world, as well as among our people and within our heritage.

Discussion Starters

- Do you think that Mendel made the right decision by leaving without telling his parents? Should he have risked his escape to find them and say goodbye or ask them to come with him?
- What were your thoughts when you found out that the other Jewish boy was Dovid?

What do you think about Mendel's choice when he turned back from the border to rescue Dovid? In what ways did this make him a "better" person? What would you have done in Mendel's place?

Activities

 Have your class draw the Pale of Settlement — the 25 provinces of Czarist Russia to which Jews were restricted from 1791 until 1917. Then have them trace Mendel's flight from Molovsk into Hungary, then Salzburg, then Hamburg, and onto the boat.

 There is a lot of mention made of herring in this book, which is a food that some of your students may never have tasted. Get both kinds, in cream sauce and plain, and have a little herring party. Serve the herring on black bread.

 To develop the idea that Papa tried to teach to Mendel — that nothing is really unconnected or exists alone — have each student figure out a way that he or she can also become a circlemaker. Lead a group discussion of this (refer primarily to Chapter 8 of *The Circlemaker*), and then have students work individually or in pairs to figure out a way to become a circlemaker.

Letters from Rifka

By Karen Hesse
Henry Holt and Company, 1992
148 pages
ISBN 0-8050-1964-2
Grades 6-8

Ms. Hesse's novel tells the story of how her Aunt Lucy came to America from Russia. Her year-long odyssey is chronicled extremely well. This is a captivating story of a wonderfully charismatic and intelligent young woman as she grows up and emigrates to a new country and a new life.

Main Ideas

- People underwent many hardships in order to emigrate to America.

- Families often had to separate, sometimes for long periods of time, in order for all members ultimately to live in America.

- People are often kind and generous, even to strangers.

Discussion Starters

- Why do you think Rifka and Saul had the kind of relationship they had? How would you describe their relationship? Would you say it was a good or bad relationship?

- What do you think was the most difficult thing Rifka had to endure, and how would you have reacted to the same situation?

- Do you think it was her experiences or her inner nature that made Rifka so helpful to others on Ellis Island? Explain your answer.

Activities

 Have each child write a letter describing his or her experiences regarding religious freedom, educational opportunities, and time to be with their family.

 Have each child cover his/her hair with a kerchief. Take a picture of each class member. Then have each bring in a picture with hair uncovered and compare the two pictures. Have them make a list of the differences between the two pictures and also describe what they think they look like in each.

 Have each child try to meet someone who emigrated to North America. Have each find out about the journey and then share all the stories.

A Time of Angels

By Karen Hesse
Hyperion Paperbacks For Children, 2000
(revised edition)
256 pages
ISBN 0-7868-0621-4
Grades 6-8

Hannah was a young teenager when World War I separated her and her two younger sisters from their parents. Their father was off at war fighting for America and their mother was stuck in Russia (where she went to care for her mother). The three girls were left with their great-aunt in a crowded tenement in Boston's West End. When the influenza pandemic (worldwide epidemic) of 1918 struck Boston, Hannah's aunt died. Hannah was then sent away from her sisters to Vermont, where she became ill. She was cared for during her recuperation by a kindly German-American farmer, who nursed her back to health and helped her return to Boston to try to find her sisters.

Main Ideas

- World War I affected many families in America and in Europe.
- There was a terrible influenza pandemic in 1918.
- Sibling love is often very strong and can overcome many obstacles.

Discussion Starters

- Do you think that the use of angels in this book was effective? Was it believable? What do you think about angels — do you think they exist? Explain your answer.

- Hannah had a great deal of responsibility for one so young, and she worked very hard. Do you know any teenagers who work as hard as she? Under what conditions do you think that you could work that hard?

Do you agree with Uncle Klaus when he says that war is always bad? Can you make an argument for war being good?

Activities

 Apple cider vinegar was talked about a lot in this book, and Uncle Klaus insisted Hannah's recuperation was based in part on her drinking it. Obtain some for your class. Drink it cold, drink it diluted with cold water, then make it with hot water and honey as Klaus did for Hannah. This should be an interesting taste experience.

 Discuss with your group any vows that they might have made — if they kept them, and if they thought the vows were effective. Help them to come up with some realistic vows for the future.

 Have your students research either the Influenza pandemic of 1918 or World War I, then make oral presentations of their findings to the group.

The Cure

By Sonia Levitan
HarperCollins Juvenile Books, 2000
180 pages
ISBN 0-380-73298-X
Grades 9-12

The imaginative writing of Sonia Levitan transforms history into a living adventure and brings to it an excitement and accessibility that would be impossible in a nonfiction book. The day-to-day life of Jews in fourteenth century Germany is vividly depicted against the backdrop of the Black Death and the tragedy of thousands of Jews who were falsely implicated in causing the widespread plague. While the historical events are dark, the stories of the individual characters are inspiring and uplifting. By reading this engrossing novel, a great deal of learning will take place.

Main Ideas

- Jewish life in Germany in the 1300s was often extremely trying.
- Prejudice has existed throughout the ages.
- The strength found in love often enabled individuals to surmount terrible situations.

Discussion Starters

- Did you find Ms. Levitan's technique of time travel effective? believable? Explain your answers.
- Was Johannes right to "trick" people out of their money at the fair, or was this just an accepted way of doing business?
- Were the Jewish people in the story brave? Support your position.

Activities

 Have each student pick a character (real or created) from the 1300s and thoroughly research the person. Then, have a day when the group comes to class as their character (e.g., in costume, speaking as though they were that person, perhaps even with "tools of the person's trade").

 Research the Black Plague in an encyclopedia or on the Internet.

 Write a time travel account ("You Are There") about one story from the Bible as a way to make the story more immediate.

Masada: The Last Fortress

By Gloria D. Miklowitz
William B. Eerdmans Publishing Co., 1999
198 pages
ISBN 0-8028-5165-1
Grades 9-12

This excellently written and engrossing historical novel brings the siege of Masada alive through a first person telling. After six years of war with Rome, the rebellious Jewish Zealots make their last stand against the mighty Roman Tenth Legion on this mountain fortress. Simon ben Eleazar, the son of the Zealot leader, and Flavius Silva, the commander of the Legion, each speak to the reader describing their experiences during the seven months of siege. Their voices breathe life into this gripping tale as it winds its way to its inevitable, horrible ending.

Main Ideas

- Jewish Zealots rebelled against Roman rule.

- The bravery and stubbornness of the Zealots was remarkable.

- The Roman government's stupidity and cruelty in how they managed the lands they conquered were also remarkable.

Discussion Starters

- Of course, the first question that must be asked is if students agree with the Zealots' premise that dying as free men is better than being enslaved and perhaps surviving to fight another day.

- Do you agree, as Simon suggests, that Aram's inability to kill demonstrated his innate humanity? Or, does it show an innate weakness?

- Which character did you find most appealing, and why?

Activities

 Construct an actual model of Masada, including the surrounding Roman camps and the ramp the Romans built. (For help, refer to the pictures inside the covers of the book and/or in other books or on the Internet.) The model will help students understand more clearly the inaccessibility of Masada and the difficulties faced by the Romans in conquering it.

 Divide the class in half and hold a debate on the first question above. Try to have students argue the point of view with which they don't agree. This will encourage them to think more deeply about their views.

 Encourage your students to have a memorial service for the Zealots who died on Masada and never received Jewish burials. (Very recently, some bones were unearthed there and buried in an Israeli military cemetery.) Have them write it themselves. They can write poetry, recite *Kaddish,* have the spirits of the dead Jews speak, etc.

For Further Reading

PK-1

All the Lights in the Night by Arthur A. Levine, illustrated by James E. Ransome. Morrow/Avon, 1991. 32 pages. ISBN 0-688-10170-0.

> This book can be used to teach about the persecution of Jews in Russia under the Czar and the story of Chanukah. Moses and his little brother Benjamin leave their small town in Russia when their older brother David sends the money for them to join him in Palestine. The story of Chanukah and their grandmother's old oil lamp sustain them on their perilous journey to freedom in the Jewish homeland. The illustrations complement the story in a wonderful way.

Grades K-2

Annushka's Voyage by Edith Tarbescu, illustrated by Lydia Dabcovich. Clarion Books, 1998. 32 pages. ISBN 0-395-64366-X.

> Annushka and Tanya are two little Jewish girls living in Russia with their grandparents in the late nineteenth century. They are waiting for their father to send them steamship tickets to America. After their mother died, he went there to make a better life for them. The tickets arrive and, taking gifts from their grandparents, they depart on their long voyage. The most important gift is their grandmother's candlesticks which she had received from her mother as a wedding present. These candlesticks come in very handy at a difficult moment for the girls and aid them in getting to their eventual reunion with their father. The illustrations are bright and joyous.

Marven of the Great North Woods written by Kathryn Lasky, illustrated by Kevin Hawkes. Harcourt Brace & Company, 1997. 48 pages. ISBN 0-15-200104-2.

> This lovely book is the true story of how Ms. Lasky's father, Marven, survived the Influenza pandemic of 1918. His parents, who emigrated from Russia to America, sent Marven, their ten-year-old son, to work as a bookkeeper in a logging camp far away from their home in Duluth, Minnesota. While living there for four months, Marven befriends an enormous French-Canadian logger named Jean Louis, and has many interesting experiences. Marven returns home after the winter to find his family has survived the influenza. Their reunion is joyful.

On the Wings of Eagles written and illustrated by Jeffrey Schrier. The Millbrook Press, Inc., 1998. 32 pages. ISBN 0-7613-0004-X.

This is the story of the dramatic rescue of the Ethiopian Jews in 1991 as experienced by one young Jewish shepherd boy. The text is complemented by unique artwork which includes line drawings, documentary photos, Judaic art, and manipulated Polaroids. The background of each page is copied from an actual *shamma* (a handwoven robe typically worn in the high mountains of Ethiopia).

Grades 2-4

Grandpa's Gamble by Richard Michelson, illustrated by Barry Moser. Marshall Cavendish, 1999. ISBN 0-7614-5034-3.

(See Featured Book, Chapter 7, "Life Cycles: To Everything There Is a Season.")

Grades 3-5

Berchick story by Esther Blanc Silverstein, pictures by Tennessee Dixon. Volcano Press, 1989. 32 pages. ISBN 0-912078-81-2.

This is the story of the unusual relationship between a Jewish woman and an orphaned colt she adopts and names Berchick. It takes place in the early 1900s and is set in the homesteading area of Wyoming. It deals with happiness, adversity, love, and the meaning of freedom. The realistic black and white illustrations bring the story to life.

Faraway Summer by Johanna Hurwitz, illustrated by Mary Azarian. Morrow Junior Books, 1998. 155 pages. ISBN 0-688-15334-8.

This chapter book tells about two weeks in the life of 12-year-old Hadassah (Dossi) Rabinowitz, a Jewish teenager living in the tenements of New York City during the summer of 1910. Her older sister, Ruthi, sends her off through the auspices of the Fresh Air Fund to live with a farm family in rural Vermont. This experience opens Dossi's mind to the outside world and to new friends. The history of the times comes alive through Dossi's eyes and words, and should keep any beginning reader interested.

Journey To America by Sonia Levitan, illustrated by Charles Robinson. Atheneum, 1993 (2nd edition). 160 pages. ISBN 0-689-31829-4.

This is the first of a trilogy about the Platt family. It begins in 1938 with Papa leaving Germany for America. He goes without Mama and their three daughters (Ruth, Lisa, and Annie), hoping that he will eventually be able to get the four of them all the necessary documentation to emigrate to America as well. While he is gone, the family must flee to Switzerland where they struggle to survive while waiting for Papa to save them. Their story is told from Lisa's perspective, which makes this a good book from which children can learn about the difficulties of that time.

Silver Days by Sonia Levitan. Econo-Clad Books, 1999. 186 pages. ISBN 0-8335-8632-7.
This is the second book in the trilogy of the Platt family. After waiting a whole year in Switzerland for Papa to send for them after their flight from Nazi Germany, the Platt family is reunited in America. The middle daughter, Lisa, once again narrates. She tells about the family's experiences as poor immigrants in early 1940s America on the eve of World War II. By the end of the book, America has entered the war. The Platts are busy helping with the war effort while adjusting to becoming Americans. This is another excellent book to teach children about a specific era, from the viewpoint of another child.

Annie's Promise by Sonia Levitan. Econo-Clad Books, 1999. 186 pages. ISBN 0-7857-9142-6.
This is the last of the Platt family trilogy by Ms. Levitan. The year is 1945, and Annie, the youngest of the three Platt girls, narrates this book as she goes through her tumultuous twelfth and thirteenth year. World War II is a presence throughout the book (and is won by the Allies by the end). Papa becomes more successful, Mama more adjusted to America, and Annie's two older sisters make their way in the world. Annie's struggles and issues explore her role as an immigrant and as a young woman living in America and provide a wonderful ending to this family saga.

Grades 4-6

After the War: The Story Behind Exodus by Carol Matas. Aladdin Paperbacks, 1997. 133 pages. ISBN 0-689-80722-8.
After having survived Buchenwald concentration camp, 15-year-old Ruth returns to her hometown to find none of her relatives there. With nowhere else to turn, she joins Brichah, an underground Jewish organization that is smuggling Jews into Palestine, and works with them in helping a group of children leave Europe. In the process, she finds that some of her relatives are still alive and she becomes reenergized. There are some very emotional passages in this book that may be difficult for some children.

Dave at Night by Gail Carson Levine. HarperCollins*Publishers*, 1999. 281 pages. ISBN 0-06-028153-7.

> This is a story set in the 1920s in the Lower East Side and Harlem. Dave, a tough 11-year-old newly orphaned Jewish boy, is placed in the Hebrew Home for Boys by his stepmother. Family relationships and friendships are explored and developed throughout this book, and Dave is certainly an engaging and fun protagonist.

Extraordinary Jewish Americans by Philip Brooks. Children's Press, 1998, 288 pages. ISBN 0-516-20609-5.

> This is an excellent reference book. It chronicles the history of Jews in America and also presents short biographies of more than 60 Jewish Americans who became famous in a variety of careers. In addition, another 124 noteworthy Jewish Americans are listed and discussed in brief at the end of the book. There are also recommendations for further reading, movies to watch, and Web sites to visit.

Israel (Cultures of the World) by Jill DuBois. Benchmark Books, 1995 (2nd edition). 128 pages. ISBN 1-85435-531-7.

> Since this reference book was written in 1995, some of Israel's recent history is obviously not included. Still, there is much valuable and historically accurate information here. Included is information about Israel's geography, history, government, economy, people, lifestyles, religions, languages, arts, leisure activities, festivals, and food.

Israel: The Founding of a Modern Nation by Maida Silverman, illustrated by Susan Avishai. Dial Books for Young Readers, 1998. 102 pages. ISBN 0-8037-2135-8.

> This is an excellent overview of the history of the land of Israel from biblical times until the establishment of the modern state. This resource book discusses all of the various rulers through the centuries, as well as many famous Jews throughout history. There is a very good time line and map at the end of the book.

The Journey Back by Johanna Reiss. Econo-Clad Books, 1999. 212 pages. ISBN 0-8335-0972-1.

> This book, the sequel to *The Upstairs Room* (see For Further Reading, Chapter 6, "Holocaust: Remembering to Remember"), chronicles the first year after World War II in Holland for Annie, her two sisters, and their father. Their painful attempts at reconstructing their lives, and the ways that they were

affected by their wartime experiences, are explored through the eyes of Annie, a 13-year-old. Ms. Reiss tells her story honestly and shows how differently people reacted to the horrors they went through and how incredibly difficult it was for all to resume "normal" lives. While many of the problems Annie and her family and friends were having are left unresolved in this story, it is still valuable reading to learn about the aftereffects of the Holocaust.

Star of Luis by Marc Talbert. Houghton Mifflin Co., 1999. 181 pages. ISBN 0-395-91423-X.

This book raises many issues — identity, family history, racism, coming of age — and presents a little known aspect of Jewish life. Through its protagonist, a young Hispanic boy named Luis, we learn about life in East Los Angeles where he and his parents live. Early in the book, Luis's father joins the army to fight in World War II and his mother receives news of her estranged father's imminent death. She and Luis return to his parents' childhood town in New Mexico. There he learns the truth about his family and their hidden Jewish heritage. Although relationships are not always well developed and the themes are not dealt with comprehensively, the book does a good job of describing this time period and these places in America.

Grades 4-8

A Kid's Catalog of Israel written and illustrated by Chaya M. Burstein. The Jewish Publication Society, 1998, 280 pages. ISBN 0-8276-0651-6.

This is an excellent resource and reference book about the land of Israel. It covers the geography, the people, the children, the story of the Diaspora, the story of Zionism and many famous Zionists, the Israeli army and many of its famous soldiers, how the Jewish holidays are celebrated in Israel, modern Hebrew, archaeology in Israel, folktales, and gives a kid's tour of Israel. Interspersed throughout are craft activities, cooking projects, songs and dances, and an extensive reading list.

Masada written and illustrated by Neil Waldman. Morrow Junior Books, 1998. 64 pages. ISBN 0-688-14481-0.

Neil Waldman has carefully researched and illustrated the entire story of Masada. He begins with its building by the mad king Herod, continues with the Jewish Zealots who fiercely defended it against the remorseless Romans who ultimately destroyed it. He then chronicles the rediscovery of this archaeologically important site and the people involved in its restoration. Mr. Waldman impartially discusses the various theories about what actually happened during the war between the Zealots and the Romans. Included are an excellent time line and glossary.

Grades 6-8

The Cross by Day, the Mezuzzah by Night by Deborah Spector Siegel. The Jewish Publication Society, 1999. 213 pages. ISBN 0-8276-0597-8.

This book is set in the Spain of 1492, and told through the story of one young girl, Isabel Caruso de Carvallo, a Catholic girl of wealth and privilege who, during the perilous times of the expulsion of the Jews, discovers that she is a Marrano (hidden Jew). How she deals with her newfound identity and her struggle to survive the political turmoil around her make for an exciting read.

Hannah Szenes: A Song of Light by Maxine Rose Schur. The Jewish Publication Society, 2000. 106 pages. ISBN 0-8276-0628-1.

Hannah Szenes, who emigrated to Palestine in 1939, was 23 years old when she was executed in 1944 in her native Hungary for being a spy for the British. She had volunteered for this role, and to accomplish it, left the safety of her country, Palestine. Her brief life and her heroism make her an unusual role model for all Jewish youth. Her poetry, which is interspersed throughout this biography, is both inspiring and instrumental in understanding her hopes and her dreams.

Moe Berg, The Spy behind Home Plate by Vivian Grey. The Jewish Publication Society, 1997. 170 pages. ISBN 0-8276-0586-2.

This biography of Moe Berg, who was one of the few Jews to play baseball in the major leagues, also details his career as a spy for the United States during World War II. He was an enigmatic athlete/scholar/spy whose accomplishments in early and middle adulthood were really quite impressive. Unfortunately, in his later years (his 50s, 60s, and early 70s) he faded into obscurity, and few today know his story. Ms. Grey details well Berg's life and the history of the times, although occasionally the book is dry.

Raoul Wallenberg: The Man Who Stopped Death by Sharon Linnea. Econo-Clad Books, 1999. 151 pages. ISBN 0-7857-2270-X.

This biography of an inspiring and incredible human being is well worth reading. Raoul Wallenberg, the Swedish architect-diplomat who saved over 100,000 Jews during the waning days of World War II, was a hero and a righteous gentile. This book documents his family history, life, and activities up until his disappearance during the last days of the war.

Remarkable Jewish Women by Emily Taitz and Sondra Henry. The Jewish Publication Society, 1996. 219 pages. ISBN 0-8276-0573-0.

Included in this reference book are over 80 portraits of Jewish women throughout history (starting with biblical times). Each is placed in the context of her historical, social, and cultural milieu. There are over 60 illustrations and photographs.

Simon Wiesenthal: Tracking Down Nazi Criminals by Laura S. Jeffrey. Enslow Publishers, 1997. 128 pages. ISBN 0-89490-830-8.

This book presents excellent overviews of World War I and World War II while interspersing Simon Wiesenthal's story and the story of the Holocaust. It also details Wiesenthal's work subsequent to the end of World War II searching down Nazi war criminals and his connection to the Museum of Tolerance in Los Angeles, which is named after him.

Yoni Netanyahu: Commando at Entebbe by Devra Newberger Speregen. The Jewish Publication Society, 1997. 120 pages. ISBN 0-8276-0642-7.

This is a biography of one of Israel's most famous soldiers, who was killed in his prime during a daring hostage rescue mission by the Israeli army. It is action packed and extremely interesting. Yoni Netanyahu was a heroic, patriotic Israeli whose heroism seems larger than life.

Grades 6 and up

Jews in America by Hasia R. Diner. Oxford University Press, 1998. 160 pages. ISBN 0-19-50678-4.

This excellent reference book is part of a 17 volume series, entitled "Religion in American Life," which explores the evolution, character, and dynamics of religion in America from the 1500s to the end of the twentieth century. This volume deals with Jews from those who first emigrated to America in 1654 until today. It provides an excellent historical overview of all of the various waves of Jewish immigration throughout the centuries, how Jews have adapted to America, and how America has adapted to the Jews. There are interesting black and white photos, pictures, and documents on almost every page which provide valuable additions to the text.

Grades 9-12

Children of Israel, Children of Palestine: Our Own True Stories edited by Laurel Holliday. Pocket Books, 1998. 358 pages. ISBN 0-67-100801-1.

This moving collection of 35 short stories is written by adults and teenagers (Israeli, Palestinian, American) who reflect on their childhood experiences in the land that both Jews and Arabs call home. This book is helpful in understanding the armed struggle between two peoples and the effects that the struggle has had on the children of both sides. Its nonpartisan manner enables the reader to get a sense of the point of view of both sides, and it provides a deeper understanding of the past and current situation in Israel.

In the Name of Sorrow and Hope by Noa Ben Artzi-Pelossof. Schocken Books, 1997. 181 pages. ISBN 0-8052-1084-9.

This is a beautifully written, love-filled memoir of Yitzhak Rabin told by his granddaughter Noa. It is deeply moving and provides a unique perspective of this famous Israeli soldier and leader. Noa reflects on her life, her country, its wars, and its deep internal divisions, and throughout makes an eloquent plea for peace for her generation.

Letters from Jerusalem, 1947-1948 by Zipporah Porath. Temple Israel, 1988. To purchase a copy, e-mail the author at zip@netvision.net.il. 233 pages. ISBN 9-65222-110-4.

These are the letters that Zipporah, a young American woman who went to Hebrew University in 1947, sent home to the United States during her first year in Israel. She intended to study for a year, but instead found herself caught up in the War of Independence. She joined the *Haganah*, the Israeli army, served as a nurse, and lived through the siege of Jerusalem. She ultimately decided to move to Israel, making *aliyah* as a result of her deep feelings for the newly established State. This is a very interesting book, especially as it is told from a woman's perspective.

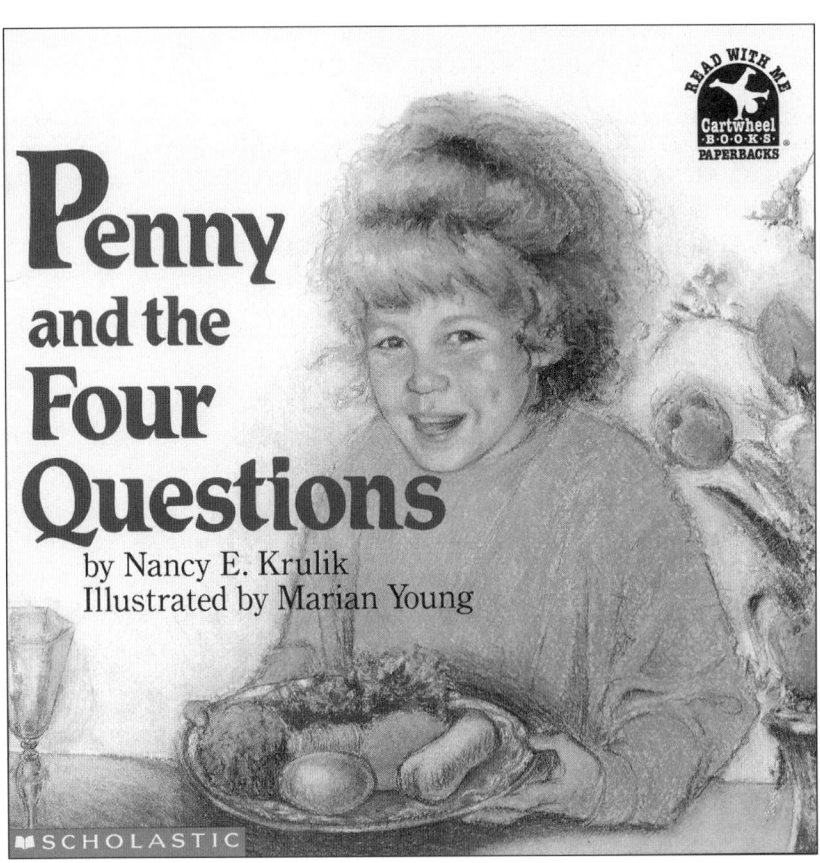

Penny
and the Four Questions

by Nancy E. Krulik
Illustrated by Marian Young

Chapter 5

Holidays: Let's Celebrate!

Every Chanukah, as we look at the faces of our families glowing in the light of the *chanukiot*, we realize yet again how joyful and meaningful a Jewish holiday can be. The holidays that we Jews observe year after year help to bind us together, while at the same time teaching us valuable life lessons. They are celebrations of freedom (Chanukah, Purim, Passover), of the earth's beauty and its bounty (Sukkot, Tu B'Shevat), the importance of rest and the demarcation of time in our lives (Shabbat), and of our obligation to others and to God (Rosh HaShanah, Yom Kippur, Shavuot). The plethora of literature that exists on the subject of the Jewish holidays is probably a testament to why the Jewish people still exists. The books that are included here are only a sampling of what is available to help us in our goal of teaching the importance and beauty of the holidays to the next generation.

Featured Books

Hanukkah (PK)
Passover (PK)
In the Month of Kislev (K-3)
Miriam's Cup (K-3)
Mrs. Moskowitz and the Sabbath Candlesticks (K-3)
Penny and the Four Questions (2-4)
When Zaydeh Danced on Eldridge Street (3-5)
The Peddler's Gift (4-6)
Esther's Story (4-6)
The Day the Rabbi Disappeared (6-8)
Passover (9-12)

Hanukkah

Written and illustrated by Miriam Nerlove
Albert Whitman & Company, 1993
24 pages
ISBN 0-8075-3142-1
PK

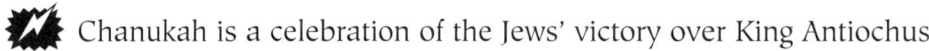

"HANUKKAH! Hanukkah's finally here! For eight nights we celebrate each year." So begins this charming and excellent introduction to Chanukah for the young child. The whole story is told in Ms. Nerlove's trademark rhyming manner, and the pictures are colorful complements. The discussion of the holiday and its customs will certainly help orient any youngster to what to expect during Chanukah. There is a glossary of Chanukah terms on the last page that the adult reader will find helpful.

Main Ideas

- Chanukah is a celebration of the Jews' victory over King Antiochus.

- After the Jewish army won, and the Temple was returned to the Jews, they relit a special light there. It is said that a miracle happened — one day's worth of oil lasted for eight days.

- There are fun foods, games, visiting with family, and presents during Chanukah.

Discussion Starters

- Besides presents, what is your favorite part of Chanukah, and why?

- Does your family have company over during Chanukah? Who comes?

- Which picture did you like the best in the book? Explain your answer.

Activities

 Make some of the foods associated with Chanukah, such as potato *latkes* or *sufganiyot* (plain or jelly filled fried doughnuts). While eating them, talk to students about why we eat foods fried in oil.

 Give each child a bag of *gelt* (chocolate money) and a *dreidel*. Teach them how to play *dreidel*.

 Make Chanukah cards for local residents of a Jewish nursing home or senior center. Make an appointment for a time when the children can deliver the cards in person. Sing a few Chanukah songs for the residents. This is always an engaging activity, one which combines the holiday with the *mitzvah* of visiting the elderly or infirm.

Passover

Written and illustrated by Miriam Nerlove
Albert Whitman & Company, 1989
24 pages
ISBN 0-8075-6360-9
PK

This is an excellent introduction to Passover for the very young child. Its rhyming sentences and simple concepts, along with the illustrations, convey the whole story in an easy and fun manner. There is a more complete explanation at the end of the book for adults. (Note: Nerlove also has written *Hanukkah* (see page 126), *Purim,* and *Shabbat* for the same audience.)

Main Ideas

- The Jews were once slaves in Egypt.
- Great miracles happened and the Jews were freed.
- We celebrate our freedom every year in the spring during the holiday of Passover.

Discussion Questions

- What is your favorite part of Passover? Is there a Passover food that you have eaten that you like a lot?
- Where are your *Sedarim* going to be this year? Who else will be there?
- What was the best part of the *Seder* in the book? Explain your answer.

Activities

 Have each child make something special that can be used at their Passover *Seder*. Some ideas are: Elijah's Cup, Miriam's Cup, *matzah* cover, *afikomen* holder, *Seder* plate, or a child's *Haggadah*.

 Bring in all different kinds of Passover food and have a food tasting. Have glasses of grape juice to drink with the food, representing the four glasses of wine we drink at the *Seder*.

 The rhyming is the most effective aspect of this book, and it contributes to its accessibility for young children. Help the children write a poem about Passover that can be copied and brought home to be used during their *Seder*.

In the Month of Kislev

By Nina Jaffe
Illustrated by Louise August
Puffin Books, 1992
32 pages
ISBN 0-670-82863-7
K-3

This is the Jewish version of Scrooge, except the holiday is Chanukah and not Christmas, and the selfish rich guy is named Feivel not Scrooge. When the poor children of Mendel the peddler "steal" the smell of the frying potato *latkes* from the house of the rich merchant Feivel, he hauls them before the Rabbi and demands retribution. He gets his fair payment in such a unique and thoughtful manner that it changes him into a previously unimaginable generous man.

Main Ideas

- The holiday of Chanukah was celebrated in Eastern Europe.

- The *mitzvah* of *tzedakah* is an important behavior to learn.

- Rabbis can provide wise solutions to problems.

Discussion Starters

- What do you think of the Rabbi's decision? Do you think he did the right thing?

- Why do you think Feivel was so selfish? Have you ever been selfish? How did you feel when you were?

- Have you and/or your family ever given *tzedakah*? To whom did you give it? What was the best thing about the experience of giving?

Activities

 What are some of your favorite smells? Close your eyes and describe them.

 Make potato *latkes* with your class and before eating them, have the children close their eyes and smell them. Using as many words as he/she can, have each child talk about the smell and describe it. Write down what each child says as he/she talks. Discuss what each came up with as you eat your *latkes*!

 Have the children bring in *tzedakah* money for every meeting/class. Save up for a worthy cause, such as planting trees in Israel through the Jewish National Fund, 42 East 69th St., New York, NY 10021, 800-542-8733, www.jnf.org.

Miriam's Cup: A Passover Story

By Fran Manushkin
Illustrated by Bob Dacey
Scholastic Press, 1998
32 pages
ISBN 0-590-67720-9
Grades K-3

Combining Bible and Midrashim, Fran Manushkin has fleshed out the story of Moses' sister Miriam for modern children. From Pharaoh's harsh decrees to the crossing of the Red Sea, Miriam the prophetess guides the Israelites. The ancient story of slavery and redemption is framed by the modern day story of a mother giving her daughter a Miriam's Cup right before the family's *Seder*.

Main Ideas

- There is a new tradition of placing a Miriam's Cup filled with water on the *Seder* table.

- Women and music play an important role in the Passover story.

- There were ten plagues visited on the Egyptians before Pharaoh allowed the Israelites to leave.

Discussion Starters

- In this book we are told of a new tradition, that of placing a cup of water on the *Seder* table to remember Miriam. What makes something a tradition? What other traditions do we follow at Passover time?

- There were ten plagues brought upon Egypt. It took a long time for Pharaoh to listen to the warnings and the plea for freedom. What if we were visited by plagues today — what kinds of plagues might they be?

- Music is such an important part of the *Seder*. What are your feelings when you sing and hear this music?

Activities

 Make a Miriam's Cup. One possibility is to take a clear plastic or glass tumbler and decorate it with puffy paints.

Look up the "Song of the Sea" in the Torah. Compare it to the surrounding text, discovering what makes it different. Read it in English.

Make drums, then learn and sing "Miriam's Song" by Debbie Friedman, which is printed on the inside covers of *Miriam's Cup*. The song is also found on the recordings *Debbie Friedman Live at the Del* and *Debbie Friedman at Carnegie Hall,* both distributed by A.R.E. Publishing, Inc., 800-346-7779, www.arepublish.com.

Mrs. Moskowitz and the Sabbath Candlesticks

Written and illustrated by Amy Schwartz
The Jewish Publication Society, 1991
32 pages
ISBN 0-8276-0372-X
K-3

When Mrs. Moskowitz and her cat Fred move into her new apartment, she is unhappy and misses her old house. Her son discovers a box she left behind and brings it to her. Inside the box is a pair of tarnished Sabbath candlesticks. She decides to clean them up and put them in a nice place. Doing so transforms her new apartment into her new home. The cute black and white drawings bring plump Mrs. Moskowitz to life.

Main Ideas

- Moving can be a very sad thing.
- Family treasures can help people get through tough times.
- Shabbat can be a time to bring your family together.

Discussion Starters

- Did you ever have anything happen to you when one thing you did just led to having to do another thing?
- Do you have Shabbat candlesticks? What do they look like?
- At the end of the book, how do you think Mrs. Moskowitz felt?

Activities

 Have children make themselves and their families a pair of Shabbat candlesticks out of clay that hardens on its own. Use Shabbat candles to fit the clay around to make these candlesticks. When the clay dries, it can be painted. Or, prior to its drying, designs could be etched in using sharp pencils.

 Teach the children the blessing over the Shabbat candles.

 Buy a prepackaged frozen *challah* and bake it with your class. Have a practice Shabbat. All share in saying the blessing over the candles, the wine (grape juice, of course), and the *challah*.

Penny and the Four Questions

By Nancy E. Krulik
Illustrated by Marian Young
Scholastic, Inc., 1993
32 pages
ISBN 0-590-46339-X
Grades 2-4

This book is an excellent introduction to Passover and its festive meal, the *Seder*. Penny is eight years old. She is very excited about having the opportunity to recite the Four Questions, which are traditionally asked by the youngest child at the *Seder*. Then she finds out that her mother has invited a family that has just moved to America from Russia. The bad news is they have a seven-year-old girl. How Penny reacts to this news, and what she learns from their *Seder* guests, illustrate the true meaning of Passover.

Main Ideas

- The Four Questions are a significant part of the *Seder*.
- The *Seder* is the festive meal of Passover, and there are many things to do to prepare for it.
- Many Russian Jews immigrated to the United States in the late twentieth century.

Discussion Starters

- How would you feel if you were Penny and your mother had just told you about Natasha? What would you say to your mother?
- Can you understand how Penny felt at the end of the book? Would you feel the same way? Explain your answer.
- Do you know anyone who will be asking the Four Questions for the first time this year? Do you think they might need help as Natasha did? Can you help them, and how?

Activities

 Study the Four Questions in Hebrew and in English. The English questions and answers can be found in the front of this book and the Hebrew version is easy to find in any traditional *Haggadah*. Help your students memorize the Four Questions, perhaps by singing them to familiar tunes.

 Help your class think of someone whose Passover they could make special and different. Have each child write down an idea, then ask parents if this is something they could actually do. If their idea is too impractical, send a note home explaining the project and ask parents to come up with an idea that is more feasible.

 Make a large mural with the Four Questions and the answers to them already written on it. Then have each child draw one picture which represents some part of one of the questions or one of the answers. Hang it in your classroom during the time that you are studying Passover.

When Zaydeh Danced on Eldridge Street

By Elsa Okon Rael
Illustrated by Marjorie Priceman
Simon & Schuster Books for Young Readers, 1997
40 pages
ISBN 0-689-80451-2
Grades 3-5

Set in the Lower East Side of Manhattan in the 1930s, this book tells the story of a young girl, Zeesie, her stern grandfather, *Zaydeh,* and the importance of Torah. Zeesie is afraid of *Zaydeh,* but when her parents go to the hospital to deliver a new baby, Zeesie must stay with her grandparents. She is reluctant but obedient, and tries to stay out of her grandfather's way. But surprise, surprise (and this is just the first of many), *Zaydeh* invites his granddaughter to join him at his synagogue to celebrate Simchat Torah. Zeesie is amazed at the beauty of the Eldridge Street Synagogue, the joy that fills its sanctuary, the yummy snacks, but most of all her grandfather dancing with the Torah. She gets her first close up look at the scroll and asks *Zaydeh,* "What is Torah?" That question leads to a new relationship between Zeesie and her grandfather and to the understanding that Torah "is the best treasure of all."

Main Ideas

- Torah is many things to many people.
- Simchat Torah is a joyous holiday.
- Relationships between grandparents and grandchildren are not always perfect and need to be worked at.

Discussion Starters

- Have you ever seen the Torah scroll close up? What were your feelings when you did? Did the scroll look as you imagined it would?

💬 If your grandparents are alive, what is your relationship with them? Do you enjoy visiting them? Is there a place in their house you especially enjoy, such as the dresser drawer filled with odds and ends that Zeesie enjoys? If your grandparents have passed away, what do you remember about them?

💬 Zayde says that he believes that Torah is a kiss from God to the Jewish people. What do you think he means by that?

Activities

👁 Look inside a Torah scroll with your group. If you can read it, let children hold the *yad* (pointer) and follow along. (If you can't, invite the Rabbi or another person who can.) Have the children describe what the Torah looks like and their thoughts as they see inside it.

🎨 It is a Simchat Torah tradition to carry a little flag with an apple stuck to the dowel. Provide the items children will need to make the flags. Display the illustrations in *When Zaydeh Danced on Eldridge Street* to give them ideas for their own flags.

🍐 Bake Bubbeh Shayndel's Apple Cake or Tante Golda's Apricot Jam Cookies (recipes in the book). Invite grandparents, uncles, and aunts to share these with you and the children.

The Peddler's Gift

By Maxine Rose Schur
Illustrated by Kimberly Bulcken Root
Dial Books for Young Readers, 1999
32 pages
ISBN 0-8037-1978-7
Grades 4-6

A young Jewish boy named Leibush in turn-of-the-century Russia relates the story of a moral decision which he faced and the quiet beloved peddler who helped him make it. The village children called the peddler Shnook because they thought he was a simpleton, but Leibush's father said that the peddler's words must be weighed and not counted. Among the peddler's wares were hand carved *dreidels* as big as a boy's fist. When one accidentally fell to the floor, Leibush pocketed it. The boy's struggle with himself, and the return of the stolen goods, make a powerful story that raises issues of honesty and prejudice. The language and illustrations vividly render another time and place. (This book can be used effectively while studying Yom Kippur or Chanukah.)

Main Ideas

- People are sometimes not what they appear to be.

- When we do something that is morally wrong, we often have the ability to correct it.

- Daily life in turn-of-the-century Russia was very different from life as we know it.

Discussion Starters

- At first, Leibush tells the peddler that he left the *dreidel* in their house, but then says, "I mean . . . I stole it." Why do you think the boy decided to be honest about what had happened, rather than taking the easier way out?

💬 What in the peddler's behavior led the children of the town to believe he was a simpleton? What happened that made Leibush change his opinion?

💬 What are the different ways in which the peddler acts with charity?

Activities

🔧 In creating this book, the author and illustrator have included many details which lend a remarkable authenticity to the story. However, these may not be things your children know about (e.g., Cossack, Evil Eye, fiery kilns, Czar, groats, oil lamp). Go through the book and list these things on a board or chart and see how many they know. Explain the others.

📄 The peddler describes the outdoors beautifully: "There is my shelter. My carpet is the road; my ceiling, the sky; and my lamps, the stars." Have each child describe their favorite place in as many words (14) and without adjectives.

🎭 Let the children act as peddlers for each other. Have them bring in objects or books that are in good shape, but with which they are ready to part. Ask them to "hawk" their wares as do the peddlers who come to the little village in the book. Instead of using money, they can trade, or they can use money that would then be used for *tzedakah*.

Esther's Story

By Diane Wolkstein
Illustrated by Juan Wijngaard
Morrow/Avon, 1998 (reprint edition)
40 pages
ISBN 0-688-15844-7
Grades 4-6

READ ALONE

This is an interesting approach to the classic Purim story. It is told in the first person by Esther. She narrates her history from before she was selected to be the queen through the tumultuous times when she saved her people. The story ends with her reflecting back on her life. It is well written, covers all of the key points, and is beautifully illustrated.

Main Ideas

- Esther is a biblical figure.
- Women can be heroes.
- Sometimes kings can do the "right" thing.

Discussion Starters

- In what ways was Esther a heroine? Was Vashti also a heroine?
- Do you think it takes more character to take action when you are afraid? Explain your answer.
- Did Mordecai control Esther, or did she do what she did because she wanted to?

Activities

 Have your class put on a Purim play. Students can rewrite the story in play form themselves. Or, they can act out the play "I Dream of Purim" in *Kings and Things: 20 Jewish Plays for Kids 8 to 18* by Meridith Shaw Patera (A.R.E. Publishing, Inc., 1996, pp. 80-92). Have them make simple costumes and scenery and invite other classes and parents for a performance.

 Make a crossword puzzle for your class using the following key words: Hadassah, Esther, Shushan, Persia, Mordecai, Ahasuerus, Megillah, Adar, Lots, Gallows, Haman, Vashti.

 Draw two large six-pointed crowns on the board. Divide the group in half. Have a trivia contest about Purim. For each question a team answers correctly, a jewel is placed on their team's crown. The first team to fill Esther's crown with jewels wins.

The Day the Rabbi Disappeared: Jewish Holiday Tales of Magic

Retold by Howard Schwartz
Illustrated by Monique Passicot
Viking Children's Books, 2000
80 pages
ISBN 0-670-88733-1
Grades 6-8

Each story in this book is a gem. Each holds sparks of magic and flames of truth. Noted folklorist Howard Schwartz has chosen tales from the oral tradition that reveal the themes of 12 Jewish holidays, including Rosh Chodesh and Shabbat. The heroes of the stories use mystical powers, but are always aware that the source of their power comes from a deep faith in God. Each story is accompanied by notes that explain many of its elements. Illustrator Monique Passicot says, "I wanted to illustrate this book because I fell in love with . . . the idea of drawing miracles." She has succeeded brilliantly.

Main Ideas

- Many Jewish stories contain elements of magic.
- The Jewish people depends on God and not magic to protect them.
- The Jewish year is filled with holiday observances.

Discussion Questions

- Have you ever heard any of these stories before? Which one(s)? Is it the same in this book as you remember it? If not, in what way is it different?
- In the story "The Cottage of Candles," there is a man who seeks justice. What do you think it means to seek justice?
- In "The Magic Wine Cup," Rabbi Pinto says, "Know that nothing happens by accident." What does he mean by that, and do you think his statement is true?

Activities

 The stories in this book come from different areas of the world with which your students may not be familiar. Tack up a world map and a map of the ancient world, and have them find the regions indicated at the end of each story. This will serve to illustrate some of the places that Jews have lived.

 There are 12 tales in this collection. Divide your group so that individuals or pairs are responsible for further researching and presenting the information given with each of the stories. They can discuss how the theme of the story relates to the theme of the holiday it illustrates. If they feel they can tell the story to the group rather than read it, invite them to do so.

 What is a Jewish holiday without food? Bring in holiday recipes from the different places mentioned in the book. Assign one to each student to make and bring in from home. Or, prepare some of the recipes as a group. As you all enjoy the treats, refer to the map, to the stories, and to the holidays.

Passover

By David Mamet
Illustrated by Michael McCurdy
St. Martin's Press, 1995
54 pages
ISBN 0-312-13141-0
Grades 9-12

Enveloped in Mamet's terse dialogue, a family's story is conveyed by a grandmother to her granddaughter. They are preparing their version of *charoset* for the upcoming family *Seder*, and are using a large knife as they work. The knife seems to prompt the girl to ask for the story about how her great-grandmother saved her family from a pogrom. Amidst the passing of many bits of family history, the grandmother relates how her ancestor in Poland tore apart her own home, then hid with the other family members under a pile of dung in order to trick the rampaging townspeople into passing by their home. The grandmother, thinking about her grandchildren, wonders, "How can they understand?" and answers herself, "They can't. Thank God."

Main Ideas

- Not that long ago, Jews were victims of pogroms.
- Family stories contain many kinds of lessons.
- The theme of Passover — freedom from bondage — can be given modern meaning.

Discussion Questions

- Does your family have anything that has been handed down through the generations like the silver candleholders in this story? Is there a story attached to it? Tell that story.

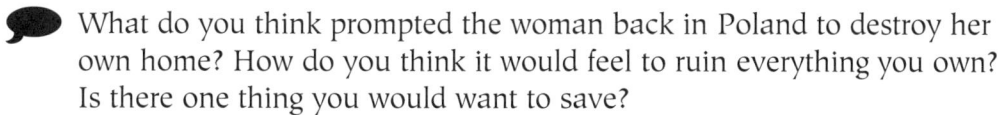 What do you think prompted the woman back in Poland to destroy her own home? How do you think it would feel to ruin everything you own? Is there one thing you would want to save?

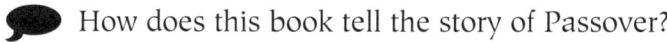 How does this book tell the story of Passover?

Activities

The very last line of the book says, " . . . and then they both turned to the sound of activity in the entranceway." Have your students write two versions of what that activity is. First, the expected — family members, a friend, a delivery person. Second, the unexpected — the police, a hateful neighbor, a telegram delivery. Have them share what they wrote. Discuss how it feels to live in our relatively safe society and what could happen to make us feel less safe.

 Make the two kinds of *charoset* recipes mentioned in the book. Have everyone taste each. Compare their flavors and consistencies and decide if one is more reminiscent of mortar then the other.

 Research the pogroms. Have the children ask their families if any of their ancestors were caught in one. Invite them to share what they find out with the class. Then they might write a prayer of thanks for the safety they enjoy today. They can use it at their family's *Seder.*

For Further Reading

PK

Beni's Family Treasury: Stories for the Jewish Holidays written and illustrated by Jane Breskin Zalben. Henry Holt & Company, Inc., 1998. 128 pages. ISBN 0-8050-5889-3.

This is a beautiful compilation of five of Ms. Zalben's classic Beni stories: "Happy New Year, Beni," "Leo & Blossom's Sukkah," "Beni's First Chanukah," "Goldie's Purim," and "Happy Passover, Rosie." In this volume Beni and his family and friends celebrate the holidays with each other. There are scenes of religious observance, traditions associated with each holiday, festive meals, family togetherness, and even some bickering among the children. This special edition has a glossary of Jewish terms and includes a ribbon marker and nameplate.

Papa's Latkes story and pictures by Jane Breskin Zalben. Henry Holt and Company, Inc., 1996. 24 pages. ISBN 0-8050-4634-8.

This is another delightful book about Beni and his family and a Jewish holiday. Because Mama is tired of making *latkes*, Papa conducts and wins a *latke* making contest. A Chanukah song and Papa's recipe are included at the end of the book. The illustrations are adorable as always.

Pearl Plants a Tree written and illustrated by Jane Breskin Zalben. Simon & Schuster Books For Young Readers, 1995. 24 pages. ISBN 0-689-80034-7.

This is a lovely extra story to have around when teaching about Tu B'Shevat, the holiday of the trees. It is about the first tree planted by Pearl's Grandpa when he came to America and the first tree Pearl helps him plant. Ms. Zalben's exceptional watercolors complement the story nicely. There is an excellent discussion of Tu B'Shevat at the end of the book, as well as other tree planting holidays, and instructions on how to plant a tree.

Sammy Spider's First Shabbat written by Sylvia A. Rouss, illustrated by Katherine Janus Kahn. Kar-Ben Copies, Inc., 1998. 32 pages. ISBN 1-58013-007-0.

This is a great introduction to Shabbat and all of its rituals, as well as an excellent review of the parts of the day. The illustrations are bold and bright and fun to look at. Sammy and his mother, Mrs. Spider, as well as the Shapiro family with whom they live, are endearing characters through which the story is told. Also in this series are: *Sammy Spider's First Hanukkah,* which teaches colors and the numbers 1 to 8; *Sammy Spider's First Passover,* which reviews basic shapes; *Sammy Spider's First Purim,* which presents different sounds; *Sammy Spider's First Rosh Hashanah,* which explores size (small, medium, large); *Sammy Spider's First Tu B'Shevat,* a December 2000 release.

Ten Good Rules by Susan Remick Topek, illustrated by Rosalyn Schanzer. Kar-Ben Copies, Inc., 1991. 32 pages. ISBN 0-929371-28-3.
   This book is an excellent adjunct to the study of Shavuot. (See Featured Books, Chapter 2, "Ethics: Doing the Right Thing.")

What Is Passover? by Harriet Ziefert, illustrated by Lillie James. Harper Festival, 1994. 16 pages. ISBN 0-694-00482-0.
   This lovely little book retells the Passover story in an easy to understand manner. Fun lift-the-flaps, under which are found pictures of many of the holiday traditions, are an added attraction, as are the delightful illustrations.

PK-1
All the Lights in the Night by Arthur A. Levine, illustrated by James E. Ransome. Morrow/Avon, 1991. 32 pages. ISBN 0-688-10170-0.
   (See For Further Reading, Chapter 4, "History: 4,000 Years and Counting.")

K-3
The Best of K'tonton by Sadie Rose Weilerstein, illustrated by Marilyn Hirsh. The Jewish Publication Society, 1988. 94 pages. ISBN 0-8276-0187-5.
   (See For Further Reading, Chapter 2, "Ethics: Doing the Right Thing.")

The Four Questions by Lynne Sharon Schwartz, illustrated by Ori Sherman. Picture Puffin, 1994 (reprint edition). 32 pages. ISBN 0-14-055269-3.
   Ori Sherman's paintings are glowingly beautiful as usual, and his use of animals all dressed up in their holiday finery is sure to engage every child who opens this book.The story, which answers the four questions traditionally asked at the Passover *Seder,* is written very clearly and is gender neutral.

The Giving Tree written and illustrated by Shel Silverstein. HarperCollins*Publishers,* 1986. 54 pages. ISBN 0-06025-665-6.
   This book is a perfect match with the study of Tu B'Shevat. (See Featured Books, Chapter 2, "Ethics: Doing the Right Thing.")

Jonah and the Two Great Fish written and illustrated by Mordicai Gerstein. Simon & Schuster Books for Young Readers, 1997. 32 pages. ISBN 0-68981-373-2.
    Because the story of Jonah is read on Yom Kippur, this book can be used when studying that holiday. (See Featured Books, Chapter 1, "Bible: In the Beginning.")

Latkes and Applesauce by Fran Manushkin, illustrated by Robin Spowart. Scholastic Inc., 1992 (reprint edition). 32 pages. ISBN 0-59042-265-0.
    This is a beautiful tale of the Menashe family who, because of a big blizzard, was unable to have *latkes* and applesauce for Chanukah. A cat and a dog wander onto their doorstep and are taken in with love by this poor family. The animals show that miracles can happen when, at the end of the storm on the last day of the holiday, they find potatoes and apples. The soft, colored chalk drawings show the cozy and loving world depicted in this book.

Mrs. Katz and Tush written and illustrated by Patricia Polacco. A Bantam Little Rooster Book, 1992. 30 pages. ISBN 0-553-08122-5.
    You can use this book when studying Passover. (See Featured Books, Chapter 2, "Ethics: Doing the Right Thing.")

The Passover Parrot written by Evelyn Zusman, illustrated by Katherine Janus Kahn. Kar-Ben Copies, Inc., 1995. 32 pages. ISBN 0-93049-430-X.
    This is a captivating story of a parrot, the latest addition to Leba's family of six siblings and two parents, who plays a major and extremely funny role in the first *Seder*. Children will love the antics of the parrot and his Hebrew speaking ability.

Pearl's Eight Days of Chanukah written and illustrated by Jane Breskin Zalben. Simon & Schuster Books For Young Readers, 1998. 40 pages. ISBN 0-689-81488-7.
    When two cousins of Pearl and Avi, Harry and Sophie, come to visit for all of Chanukah, anything can and does happen. The eight stories about their holiday together and the wonderful activities and experiences they share are very well done and beautifully illustrated. There is a wide variety of excellent and age appropriate crafts, games, songs, and recipes to help enhance a child's holiday experience.

The Sabbath Lion: A Jewish Folktale from Algeria retold by Howard Schwartz and Barbara Rush, illustrated by Stephen Fieser. HarperTrophy, 1996 (reprint). 32 pages. ISBN 0-06-44382-X.
    (See Featured Books, Chapter 3, "Folklore: From Generation To Generation.")

The Shadow of a Flying Bird: A Legend from the Kurdistan Jews retold and illustrated by Mordicai Gerstein. Hyperion Books for Children, 1994. 32 pages. ISBN 0-7868-0016-X.

This book relates the last days of Moses' life as told in Midrashim about the last verses of the Torah. Therefore, it is appropriate for use when preparing for Simchat Torah. (See Featured Books, Chapter 1, "Bible: In the Beginning.")

The Two Brothers: A Legend of Jerusalem retold and illustrated by Neil Waldman. Atheneum Books for Young Readers, 1997. 40 pages. ISBN 0-689-31936-3.

This story can be used effectively when studying Tishah B'Av. (See Featured Books, Chapter 3, "Folklore: From Generation To Generation.")

The World's Birthday: A Rosh Hashanah Story by Barbara Diamond Goldin, illustrated by Jeanette Winter. Turtleback, 1995. 32 pages. ISBN 0-606-10086-5.

Young Daniel knows that Rosh HaShanah is coming soon and he wants to throw a birthday party for the world. His older sister Naomi is skeptical, but she accompanies him to the bakery where he buys the largest cake. They then go to their grandfather to see if he knows what to do at such a party. While creating a big card to wish the world and everyone a good New Year, Daniel figures out just how to celebrate. The party is a great success. Even Naomi agrees!

Grades 2-4

The Carp in the Bathtub by Barbara Cohen, illustrated by Joan Halpern. Econo-Clad Books, 1999 (reissue). 48 pages. ISBN 0-78575-042-8.

This endearing and enduring classic, originally published in 1972, tells the story of Leah and Harry and their ongoing friendships with all of the fish their mother buys to make into gefilte fish for the Jewish holidays. In particular, it is about their special relationship with a carp they name Joe. Their attempt to rescue him from the terrible fate of being the famous gefilte fish appetizer makes for a hilarious, bittersweet, and moving story. The black and white drawings bring these two mischievous children and their dilemma to life.

Hershel and the Hanukkah Goblins by Eric Kimmel, illustrated by Trina Schart Hyman. Holiday House, 1989. 32 pages. ISBN 0-8234-0769-1.

Just as the Syrians attempted to eradicate Jewish worship in ancient Jerusalem, a group of goblins has made it impossible for the Jews of a little Eastern European village to celebrate Chanukah. But along comes Hershel of Ostropol, a hero of Jewish folklore, to save Chanukah. On each of the first seven nights, Hershel is able to light the Chanukah *menorah* in the old deserted synagogue by playing tricks on the goblins who try to stop him. On the eighth night, Hershel comes face to face with the King of the Goblins. Through one last very brave and clever ruse, Hershel assures that the spirit of Chanukah will prevail.

How Yussel Caught the Gefilte Fish: A Shabbos Story by Charlotte Herman, illustrated by Katya Krenina. Dutton Children's Books, 1999. 40 pages. ISBN 0-525-45449-7.

This story captures all of the lovely traditions and family togetherness that Shabbat represents in Judaism. The main story line tells of Yussel going fishing for the first time with his father. They plan to catch the fish Yussel's mother will use to make gefilte fish for their Sabbath dinner. The three fish Yussel catches each cause exciting battles (and remind him and his father of various relatives). They contribute wonderfully to the story, as well as to the meal.

The Magician's Visit: A Passover Tale by Barbara Diamond Goldin, illustrated by Robert Andrew Parker. Turtleback, 1995. 32 pages. ISBN 0-606-07827-4.

With this book, Goldin has beautifully retold a holiday tale by Yiddish writer I.L. Peretz. Beginning with its first line, "A magician came to town," the reader is charmed by a miraculous story of a mysterious stranger who helps a poor pious couple celebrate Passover. Its message of faith and charity is a vital one to explore with children.

Raisel's Riddle by Erica Silverman, illustrated by Susan Gaber. Farrar, Straus and Giroux, 1999. 40 pages. ISBN 0-374-36168-1.

Add this book to your study of Purim. (See Featured Books, Chapter 3, "Folklore: From Generation To Generation.")

Grades 3-5

The Magic of Kol Nidre: A Yom Kippur Story by Bruce H. Siegel, illustrated by Shelly O. Haas. Kar-Ben Copies, Inc., 1998. 32 pages. ISBN 1-58013-002-X.

Traditionally, the *"Kol Nidre"* prayer is chanted three times. It is sung once softly, then with normal volume, and finally loudly. When he is a young boy, the narrator's grandfather tells him there is magic in the prayer, but that the boy must find out what it is for himself. When the narrator is himself a young father, he again wonders what the magic is. And finally, when he is a grandfather, he understands that it is sung first for our ancestors, then for ourselves, and finally for the generations yet to be. Siegel has written a thoughtful and powerful message of continuity and the sacredness of the *"Kol Nidre"* prayer.

Molly's Pilgrim by Barbara Cohen, illustrated by Daniel Mark Duffy. Lothrop, Lee and Shepard, 1998 (revised edition). 32 pages. ISBN 0-688-16279-7.
    You can use this book while studying Sukkot. (See Featured Books, Chapter 4, "History: 4,000 Years and Counting.")

One Yellow Daffodil: A Hanukkah Story by David A. Adler, illustrated by Lloyd Bloom. Voyager Books, 1999. 32 pages. ISBN 0-15-20294-2.
    (See For Further Reading, Chapter 6, "The Holocaust: Remembering to Remember.")

There's No Such Thing as a Chanukah Bush, Sandy Goldstein by Susan Sussman, illustrated by Charles Robinson. Albert Whitman & Company, 1983. 48 pages. 0-8075-7863-0.
    Robin, a young Jewish girl, grapples with the overwhelming presence of Christmas and the issue of Christmas trees in Jewish homes. She decides to ask her mother for a "Chanukah Bush," and is told there is no such thing. Her mother explains that there are many different ways of being Jewish. Robin's Grandpa gets involved, and brings Robin along as his guest to his union's Christmas party. They have a wonderful time, but afterward Robin asks why it is all right for them to go to a Christmas party, but not all right for them to have a Christmas tree. Grandpa helps her understand the difference between doing something because you believe in it and helping someone else celebrate their holiday. This is a good book from which to launch a discussion about the "December dilemma" and also about tolerance for the beliefs of others.

Grades 4-6

The Christmas Menorahs: How a Town Fought Hate by Janice Cohn, illustrated by Bill Farnsworth. Albert Whitman & Company, 1995. 40 pages. ISBN 0-8075-1152-8.
    (See Featured Books, Chapter 2, "Ethics: Doing the Right Thing.")

Dear Elijah by Miriam Bat-Ami. Farrar Straus Giroux, 1995. 106 pages. ISBN 0-374-31755-0.
    Use this book when studying Passover. (See For Further Reading, Chapter 7, "Life Cycle: To Everything There Is a Season.")

The Uninvited Guest and other Jewish Holiday Tales by Nina Jaffe, illustrated by Elivia. Scholastic, Inc. 1993. 72 pages. ISBN 0-590-44653-3.
    In this festive collection, Nina Jaffe has drawn on different folktales and legends to enliven seven different holidays — Rosh HaShanah, Yom Kippur,

Sukkot, Chanukah, Purim, Passover, and Shabbat. Each story is introduced with a little bit about the history and observance of the holiday. The book ends with source notes, a brief explanation of the Jewish calendar, a glossary, and suggestions for further reading.

While the Candles Burn: Eight Stories for Hanukkah by Barbara Diamond Goldin, illustrated by Elaine Greenstein. Viking, 1996. 60 pages. ISBN 0-670-85875-7.
Eight themes of Chanukah — faith, miracles, traditions, religious commitment, peace, honoring women, charity, and rededication — are examined in the stories in this book. The last story in this collection is original; the others are retold from classic sources. These tales will provoke many questions for discussion.

Who Knows Ten: Children's Tales of the Ten Commandments by Molly Cone, illustrated by Robin Brickman. UAHC Press, 1997 (revised edition). 112 pages. ISBN 0-80740-080-7.
This book is ideal for use when studying Shavuot. (See Featured Books, Chapter 2, "Ethics: Doing the Right Thing.")

Grades 6-8

The Passover Journey: A Seder Companion by Barbara Diamond Goldin, illustrated by Neil Waldman. Viking, 1994. 56 pages. ISBN 0-670-82421-6.
The first part of this handsome volume provides a narrative of the Exodus, from the Israelites' life in Egypt to the crossing of the Sea of Reeds. It is beautifully crafted using The Jewish Publication Society translation of the book of Exodus and classic Midrashim. The second part of the book discusses the *Seder* and its 14 steps. The book includes Sephardic and Oriental customs for the telling of the story, and a section of background on the Warsaw Ghetto (another *mitzrayim*, a word that can be translated as "Egypt" or "narrow place"). This is a thoughtful and attractively illustrated addition to the study of Passover.

The Violin Players by Eileen Bluestone Sherman. The Jewish Publication Society, 1998. 121 pages. ISBN 0-8276-0595-1.
This book is an excellent compliment to the study of Purim. (See Featured Books, Chapter 2, "Ethics: Doing the Right Thing.")

Grades 9-12

Jewish Days: A Book of Jewish Life and Culture around the Year by Francine Klagsbrun, illustrated by Mark Podwal. The Noonday Press, 1996. 232 pages. ISBN 0-374-17923-9.

Elie Weisel called this book "A blessed combination of two remarkable talents, thirsting for wonder, and imagination." Month by month, *Jewish Days* discusses the significant days in the Jewish calendar — holidays, historical events, biblically dated events, and biographical data. Each month is introduced with information about the kabbalists' interpretation of its zodiac sign. Mark Podwal's fanciful line drawings and full color illustrations make this book a visual treasure.

All Ages

Beni's Family Cookbook for the Jewish Holidays written and illustrated by Jane Breskin Zalben. Henry Holt and Company, 1996. 91 pages. ISBN 0-8050-3735-7.

This is a sumptuous collection of recipes for every Jewish holiday through the year. Also included are notes on the religious and cultural importance of each holiday and amusing introductory notes to each recipe. Many of the recipes are healthier updates of old classics (e.g., low cholesterol *matzah* balls, vegetarian chopped liver) and appear extremely easy to follow. The illustrations are classic Ms. Zalben and grace each page with a scene from the life of Beni and his family.

The Kids' Catalog of Jewish Holidays by David A. Adler. The Jewish Publication Society. 1996. 283 pages. ISBN 0-8276-0581-1.

Here is an entertaining collection of material from around the world, including information about each Jewish holiday, international customs, the story of the Jewish calendar, stories, poems, recipes, songs, crafts, cartoons, word puzzles, riddles, and further resources. This is an excellent source book for parents and teachers to help in spicing up the various holidays, and as an aid to informal Jewish education.

The Family Treasury of Jewish Holidays by Malka Drucker, illustrated by Nancy Patz. Little, Brown, and Company, 1994. 180 pages. ISBN 0-316-19313-5.

This book is chock full of stories, facts, and activities from around the world through which to celebrate all of the Jewish holidays. There are ten chapters, all of which include the history and rituals of each holiday and a read-aloud section of stories by a variety of authors. In addition, each chapter includes a related song, recipe, or craft.

Milk and Honey: A Year of Jewish Holidays by Jane Yolen, illustrated by Louise August. Musical arrangements by Adam Stemple. G.P. Putnam's Sons, 1996. 80 pages. ISBN 0-399-22652-4.

    This is an excellent family and school reference book about the Jewish year of holidays and celebrations which commemorate our history and beliefs. Ms. Yolen leads us through the year starting with the Days of Awe, continuing with Sukkot, Chanukah, Purim, Passover, and Shavuot, and ending with a section on Shabbat. She gives the history and customs of each holiday, and includes stories, poems, and songs accompanied by easily played music for piano and guitar. The illustrations are beautiful, old fashioned, and evocative of the various holidays.

To Every Thing There Is a Season: Verses from Ecclesiastes illustrated by Leo and Diane Dillon. Scholastic, Inc., 1998. 30 pages. ISBN 0-590-47887-7.

    Traditionally, Ecclesiastes is read on Sukkot. (See For Further Reading, Chapter 7, "Life Cycles: To Everything There Is a Season.")

Chapter 6

The Holocaust: Remembering to Remember

Most of us remember the horror we experienced when we first learned about the Holocaust. Ellen was in the family car traveling from her home in Pennsylvania to relatives in New York. She looked out the window at the factories and refineries that punctuate the New Jersey Turnpike as it approaches New York. Watching the smoke curl from one of the smoke stacks, she was momentarily transported to the horrors of the death camps. She suddenly felt overwhelming grief, and choked on her tears. She was quite young, perhaps ten years old, and had not yet read any of the vast literature about the Holocaust. But that defining moment set the stage for years of inquiry and mourning. In this chapter, you will find a selection of books for children and young adults that addresses the events of that most sorrowful time in our Jewish experience.

Featured Books

Terrible Things (1-4)
The Lily Cupboard (2-5)
The Feather Bed Journey (3-5)
The Number on My Grandfather's Arm (3-5)
Passage To Freedom (3-5)
The Devil's Arithmetic (4-6)
The Night Crossing (4-6)
Number the Stars (4-6)
The Hidden Children (6-8)
I Never Saw Another Butterfly (6 and up)
Night (9-12)
No Pretty Pictures (9-12)

Note regarding Holocaust: "According to the dictionary, [it] means destruction, devastation, total consummation by fire. Today, the word refers specifically to what is surely one of the darkest periods in history, the years of terror during which one nation and its leader — Nazi Germany and Adolf Hitler — tried by all possible means to annihilate the Jews of Europe, and succeeded in destroying six million of them." (From the *Hidden Children* by Howard Greenfeld)

Kristallnacht (Night of the Broken Glass) refers to the anti-Jewish outrage in Germany and Austria that began on the evening of November 9, 1939 and continued through the night. During that terrible night, many windows of synagogues and Jewish owned stores were smashed, then burned and looted. Over 30,000 Jews were arrested and sent to concentration camps. Many others were beaten and otherwise terrorized. Some 36 were killed.

KAREN ACKERMAN

THE Night Crossing

Her freedom depended on it...

illustrated by ELIZABETH SAYLES

Terrible Things: An Allegory of the Holocaust

By Eve Bunting
Illustrations by Stephen Gammell
The Jewish Publication Society, 1996
32 pages
ISBN 0-8276-0325-8
Grades 1-4

This allegory of the Holocaust is one of the few books to convey some of the horror of that time in a way that can be comprehended by very young children without frightening them. The "Terrible Things" come for one species after another until all are gone, except Little Rabbit, who goes to another forest to warn the animals who live there. He hopes they will believe him and perhaps do something, unlike the animals in the other forest. Ms. Bunting very clearly encourages children to stand up for what they think is right, even if they are alone in their beliefs.

Main Ideas

- Terrible things can happen if people don't act to stop them.
- People sometimes try to do what is easiest, not what is right.
- Always try to do what you think is right.

Discussion Starters

- What could the animals have done differently?
- Why did the different animals not really answer Little Rabbit's questions?
- If you were Little Rabbit, would you have been afraid? Why or why not?

Activities

 Have each child make a drawing of what they think the Terrible Things look like. As a group, talk about the drawings.

 Have the class make a list of things that are important to them and worth sticking up for. Help them think of ways they can stand up for those things.

 To give students the experience of seeing a wrong and being able to correct it, have them think about one thing they can do that will solve a problem. Teach them that they have the power to be morally correct.

The Lily Cupboard: A Story of the Holocaust

By Shulamith Levey Oppenheim
Illustrated by Ronald Himler
Econo-Clad books, 1999
32 pages
ISBN 0-7857-6096-2
Grades 2-5

In the gentlest possible way, the author presents the story of Miriam, a young Jewish girl whose parents send her away to live in safety with a non-Jewish family in the countryside of Holland. Set within the historical framework of the war and its threat to Jews, the story unfolds when her parents prepare Miriam for their separation. Mother asks her to select one doll to bring. When Miriam says that the family has to stay together, she expresses every child's wish. Although the threat of the German soldiers is very real in the book, they are never graphically depicted, and Miriam is kept safe throughout the narrative.

Main Ideas

- The Germans threatened the safety of Jews in Holland in 1940.
- Some Jewish children were sent to live with non-Jewish families.
- The separation of parents from their children is very sad.

Discussion Starters

- Why do you think Miriam was so attached to the rabbit that Nello gave her?
- It is fun to play the game *Hide and Seek*. What is different about the kind of hiding Miriam and others had to do during the war?
- How do you think Miriam's parents felt about sending her away?

Activities

 Ask the children to choose what they would take along if they were going away to live with other people for a while. Bring a small suitcase to class to demonstrate the space available to them. Have them share their conclusions with you and the rest of the class. You can make a list on the blackboard for all to see.

 The author has chosen not to tell us what happened to Miriam, Nello, his parents, or Miriam's parents. Have your group write or dictate what they think happened to the characters in the book in the years that followed.

 When danger approaches, Miriam is hidden in a cupboard painted with lilies. Bring in a vase of lilies and have the children paint watercolors of them. Provide good quality watercolor paper, brushes, paints, and pencils.

The Feather Bed Journey

By Paula Kurzband Feder
Illustrated by Stacey Schuett
Albert Whitman & Co., 1995
32 pages
ISBN 0-8075-2330-5
Grades 3-5

This is an excellent introduction to the Holocaust in Poland. Through the telling of the history of a special pillow, a grandmother teaches her two grandchildren about both the evil and the good that occurred during that time.

Main Ideas

- Children were hidden and saved during the Holocaust.
- Family heirlooms tell a family's stories and are very important.
- Children can learn a lot by listening to their grandparents.

Discussion Starters

- How do you think Rachel and Lewis felt about ripping the pillow after they heard Grandma's story?
- Do you or your family own anything special like the pillow in this story? Tell about it.
- Who do you think was braver: the farmer (Jan Witkowski) or the child he hid who became Grandma?

Activities

- Invite a survivor who was a hidden child to speak to the children.

- Visit a Holocaust museum or memorial.

- Have children bring in something from home that is part of a family story and have them show it and tell about it. This session would be especially meaningful if some grandparents could participate.

The Number on My Grandfather's Arm

By David Adler
Photographs by Rose Eichenbaum
UAHC Press, 1987
28 pages
ISBN 0-8074-0328-8
Grades 3-5

In the security of her own home, a young girl is introduced to the Holocaust. In very simple language, her grandfather, a survivor, tells how in the eyes of the Nazis, "We were no longer people . . . We were numbers." He describes how Jews were treated by the Germans and a little bit about the concentration camps. After hearing the story for the first time, the child tries to comfort her grandfather. The photographs in this book illustrate the story that is going on in the girl's house, and also include photos from Europe at the time of the Nazis.

Main Ideas

- Not that long ago, there was a period of horrific anti-Semitism in Europe.

- The Nazi's treated some people as if they were numbers, not people.

- Many people were killed, but some survived.

Discussion Starters

- Why do you think the young girl's mother and grandfather decide it's time for her to hear about what happened to the Jews in Europe when her grandfather was young? Why do you think her grandfather wanted to avoid talking to her about it?

- What do you think Grandpa meant when he said, "We were no longer people to them. We were numbers"?

- How do you think the girl feels hearing about what happened to her grandfather? What did she do about it? How do you think her mother feels?

Activities

 Have the children say in one word how they feel upon reading this book. Write these feeling words on the board. Also have them imagine, and describe in one word, how Grandfather felt during the war and how he feels telling his story to his granddaughter. Add those words to the board. Compare and contrast these lists.

 View and discuss the animated video *Sarah and the Squirrel,* one of the few films that makes the Holocaust accessible to young children. Sarah is alone and terrified in the forest after her family disappears, but with the help of some very special animals, she learns how to survive. The video is available from the Board of Jewish Education of Greater New York, 212-245-8200, ext. 316.

 Do some role playing. One child acts out feeling sad/angry/lost, etc., and the others try to comfort him/her.

Passage To Freedom: The Sugihara Story

By Ken Mochizuki
Illustrated by Dom Lee
Afterword by Hiroki Sugihara
Lee & Low Books, Inc., 1997
32 pages
ISBN 1-88000-049-0
Grades 3-5

This book is written from Hiroki Sugihara's five-year-old point of view. In 1940, his father was a Japanese diplomat stationed in Lithuania. One morning, a crowd of Polish Jewish refugees gathered outside the family's house. They were requesting visas to Japan so that they could escape certain death at the hands of the approaching Nazis. Three times, Chiune Sugihara requested permission to issue these visas, and three times the Japanese government refused. Then the family took matters into their own hands, and decided they would do what they could to save these Jews. For over a month, there was a line of refugees at their home, and every day Sugihara wrote 300 visas. In an afterword, Hiroki Sugihara describes the family's hardships following this act of heroism. He concludes, "It is a story that proves that one person can make a difference."

Main Ideas

- Sometimes a person must take a risk to do what is right.

- One person can make a difference.

- During the Holocaust, the Jews turned to many people for help.

Discussion Starters

- Do you think that Chiune Sugihara made the right decision given the way he was treated after leaving Lithuania? (See the afterword.) Do you think you would be able to take such a risk? Why or why not?

💬 There is a Jewish proverb at the beginning of the book: "If you save the life of one person, it is as if you saved the world entire." What does this mean? How does this proverb relate to this book? There is also a Japanese proverb: "Even a hunter cannot kill a bird that comes to him for refuge." What does this mean? How does it relate to this book?

💬 Why do you think the Sugihara family was brave enough to take a risk and help the Jews?

Activities

 Hiroki Sugihara is still alive, and lives in San Francisco. Have your class write him letters in appreciation of what his family did. Send the letters to him c/o Lee and Low Books, 95 Madison Ave., Suite #606, New York, NY 10016.

 Instruct each child to write his/her own names over and over again for ten minutes. Then have them figure out how long it would have taken Chiune Sugihara to write his name 300 times a day, and how many times he would have signed his name in a month. Imagine what that must have been like for him.

 Find out more about Yad Vashem in Israel and the Hill of Humanity in Japan. Use an encyclopedia or the Internet.

The Devil's Arithmetic

By Jane Yolen
Econo-Clad, 1999
170 pages
ISBN 0-67081-027-4
Grades 4-6

Hannah is a typical 12-year-old American girl who is bored by the Passover *Seder* and by her parents' and grandparents' overbearing need to remember. When she opens the door for Elijah, Hannah is transported back to the 1940s and a Polish *shtetl* (Jewish town). What she learns during the time she lives as Chaya, a Polish Jewish girl, teaches her about the horrors of the Holocaust and the importance of remembering. (When using this book, you might want to obtain *The Devil's Arithmetic: A Unit Plan* by Jane Sherman, published by Teacher's Pet Publications, 1998.)

Main Ideas

- Our Jewish traditions are designed to help us remember our past.
- The concentration camps of World War II were filled with horrors.
- Females and males had different experiences during the Holocaust.

Discussion Starters

- Why do you think it is important to remember our history? Would it be better just to forget about bad things?
- What did you find to be the scariest part of this book? Why?
- With which person in the book did you most closely identify? Why?

Activities

 On a blackboard or big piece of paper, make a list of all the Jewish holidays. Have students come up with their reason for remembering each holiday (e.g., what it means to their family, or what that holiday represents). Make a list of all the reasons to remember each holiday.

 Have each student ask their parents after whom he/she was named or why they were given their name. Relate it to the reason Hannah was named after her Aunt Eva's friend who died in the concentration camp.

 View and discuss the movie *Yentl* with your students. This will give them insight into what life was like in the *shtetl*, as well as the differences in how boys and girls were raised, especially when it came to education. You can also rent from a video store the film *The Devil's Arithmetic*, which is based on this book.

The Night Crossing

By Karen Ackerman
Illustrated by Elizabeth Sayles
Random House Children's Publications, 1995
(reprint edition)
58 pages
ISBN 0-679-87040-7
Grades 4-6

This is a docu-novel of a young girl, Clara, and her family's escape from Nazi occupied Austria. Because the father of this family is convinced that it will not be safe for Jews under the Germans, he sells all of the family's valuables in order to buy safety for their journey to the Swiss border. Clara's mother, however, refuses to allow him to sell her silver candlesticks. The story of how the family of four, along with the precious candlesticks, make it to safety can serve as an excellent introduction to the Holocaust.

Main Ideas

- Some Jewish families did leave Nazi occupied Europe before it was too late.
- It is difficult to leave places and things behind.
- People risked their own safety, often for a price, to help escapees.

Discussion Starters

- How was Clara's escape from the Nazi's like her grandmother's escape from the Cossacks?
- Why do you think more people did not leave their homes and countries as the Nazis came to power?
- Did you guess they would hide the candlesticks in the two dolls that Clara carries with her? What clues were in the story to lead you to that conclusion?

Activities

Tell the children the history of your own candlesticks, then ask them to find out the history of theirs. Ask them to bring their candlesticks to class and share the stories behind them. (Help children who don't have a pair of candlesticks to make a pair and thus start their own tradition.) Teach the *brachah* over the candles, as well as how to cover the eyes while reciting it. Explain the tradition behind this act.

The swastika appears in a couple of the illustrations in this book. Have your students research its origin and meaning. Use an encyclopedia or the Internet.

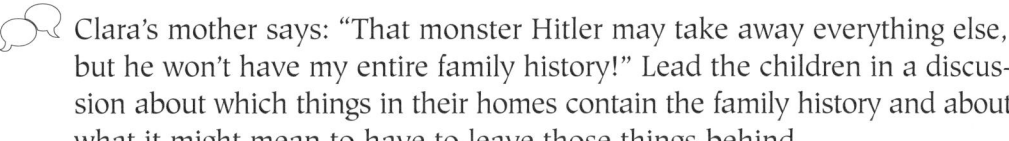
Clara's mother says: "That monster Hitler may take away everything else, but he won't have my entire family history!" Lead the children in a discussion about which things in their homes contain the family history and about what it might mean to have to leave those things behind.

Number the Stars

By Lois Lowry
Yearling Books, 1990 (reissue edition)
137 pages
ISBN 0-440-40327-9
Grades 4-6

READ ALONE

This account of the Jews' escape in 1943 from Nazi occupied Copenhagen is told through the eyes of a young non-Jewish school girl, Annemarie. The story begins on the eve of the Nazi plan to relocate the Jews, and follows the successful escape of the Rosen family, which is aided by Annemarie's family and by members of the Resistance. The story is an examination of the meaning of bravery and courage.

Main Ideas

 Denmark, under the leadership of King Christian X, saved its Jewish population.

 A person can be afraid yet brave at the same time.

 Ordinary people can perform acts of courage.

Discussion Starters

In the beginning of the story, Annemarie thinks that ordinary people like the Rosens, and her own family, the Johansens, would never be called upon to be courageous. Is this true? Can you think of other times when ordinary people act courageously?

Who do you think the bravest person in this book is? Explain your answer.

Before Uncle Henrik explained it at the end of the book, what did you think was in the package that Mr. Rosen was supposed to pass to Henrik?

Activities

 Divide the class into work groups and assign one of the following research topics for each group to present visually to the rest of the class:

1. The geography of Denmark
2. The history of the Jews in Denmark
3. The role King Christian X played in saving Denmark's Jews during World War II

 Give the group time to think about what a reunion between Ellen and Annemarie would be like if they met after the war. Have each student write out their thoughts as an ending or epilogue to the book. They can share these with each other and perhaps you can send them to the author: Lois Lowry, c/o Random House Children's Books, 1540 Broadway, New York, NY 10036.

 The title of this book comes from Psalm 147. Peter reads part of it during a moment of extreme danger in the story. Read the Psalm with your group and discuss its meaning.

The Hidden Children

By Howard Greenfeld
Houghton Mifflin Company, 1997
118 pages
ISBN 0-395-86138-1
Grades 6-8

During the Holocaust, one and a half million Jewish children were murdered. This is now a familiar statistic. Here's another number to consider: between 10,000 and 100,000 Jewish children were hidden and survived. Greenfeld artfully weaves the history of this era with the oral histories of 13 of those children. The book is illustrated with photos, which help one to imagine what it might have been like for these individuals. Some children were adopted by Christian families or taken in by orphanages. Some hid in haystacks and attics, and others survived in the woods. They all lived to tell their stories, and now it is up to others to remember them.

Main Ideas

- Some Jewish children survived the war by being hidden.

- Those who protected these children were not always kind.

- After liberation, these children faced many kinds of difficulties.

Discussion Starters

- Imagine that you, too, lived during the Holocaust. Where would you choose to hide — in an orphanage, a convent, with a family, in an attic, in the woods? Explain your answer.

- Many of the people in Howard Greenfeld's book talk about the loneliness of their situation. Who are the people in your life that you would miss the most if you were in this situation?

- We are told that the people in this book are all high achievers. Why do you think this is so?

Activities

 Have each child pick one of the photos in the book, then write a story about where the people in the photo are coming from and where they are going. Also, have them imagine the person who took the picture and how he or she fits into the story.

 One of the survivors interviewed for this book is chemist and Nobel Prize winner Roald Hoffmann. Find out more about him, then read some of his poetry in his book *Memory Effects,* Calhoun Press, 1999.

 Research the work of The Jewish Foundation for the Righteous, 305 7th Ave., New York, NY 10001, 212-727-9955, www.jfr.org. This organization financially supports many individuals who hid or rescued Jews during World War II. They also have a Speakers Bureau. Perhaps your synagogue or organization can sponsor a visit by a rescuer or survivor through this organization.

I Never Saw Another Butterfly: Children's Drawings and Poems from Terezin Concentration Camp, 1942-1944

Edited by Hana Volavkova
Pantheon Books, 1993 (2nd expanded edition)
106 pages
ISBN 0-8052-4115-9
Grades 6 and up

Fifteen thousand children under the age of 15 passed through the Terezin Concentration Camp. Less than 100 survived. Shortly after the war's end, Willy Groag, a former prisoner of Terezin, brought two suitcases filled with the drawings and poems of the young inmates to the authorities in the Jewish community of Prague. For ten years, the filled suitcases were ignored. Now they are honored all over the world through exhibits of the works and also through this book, which was originally published in 1964.

Main Ideas

- Hardships sometimes sharpen our appreciation for things often taken for granted.

- Even under the worst conditions, people have the urge and the ability to create things of beauty.

- Jewish children were killed during the Holocaust.

Discussion Starters

- Which poem and/or picture do you like the best, and why? Of what does it remind you?

- Why do you think the Nazi's established this "model ghetto"?

- Why did Freidl Dicker-Brandeis risk her own safety to teach art to the children of Terezin when there was no chance for survival?

Activities

Note: The activities below have been adapted with permission from *Jewish Literature for Children: A Teaching Guide* by Suzy Engman and Cheryl Silberberg Grossman (A.R.E. Publishing, Inc., 1985).

 Sit with your group in a beautiful, grassy, flowering garden or under a shade tree. Have students take turns reading the poems in the book out loud.

 Have each student make a crayon etching to serve as a symbolic representation of the bleakness of the Holocaust and the dreams, which the children of Terezin allowed to shine through. Using crayons, brightly color every part of a piece of white oak tag. Then, using a black crayon or India ink, cover the entire sheet again. Take a sharp tool and etch out a picture, such as a flower, a bird, or a butterfly. Have each child describe what it was like to move aside the dark to allow the bright colors through, then relate it to the experiences described in the book. (Protect your work area with newspaper.)

 Research Terezin in an encyclopedia or on the Internet.

Night

By Elie Wiesel
Bantam Books, 1982 (reissue edition)
109 pages
ISBN 0-553-27253-5
Grades 9-12

Originally published in French in 1958, and in English in 1960, *Night* was called by *The New York Times* "a slim volume of terrifying power." In it, Nobel Laureate Elie Wiesel describes in detail the sights he witnessed as a teenager during the Holocaust. The book is an elegant call to all who read it that such inhumanity must never be allowed to happen again. Please note that this book should not be used as an introduction to the Holocaust. *Night* is also available as *The Night Trilogy: Night, Dawn, The Accident* from Farrar, Straus & Giroux, 1987.

Main Ideas

- During the horrible stages along the way, the victims of the Holocaust did not know what lay before them.

- When facing the inferno, some Jews clung to their faith; others rejected it.

- We must study the past for the sake of our future.

Discussion Starters

- Why is it important to remember the Holocaust?

- Why do you suppose some Jewish victims clung to their faith? Why do you suppose some revolted against God? Which do you think you might have done?

- About halfway through the book, Mr. Wiesel says, "Their parents, like mine, had lacked the courage to wind up their affairs and emigrate while there was still time." Do you think this was a matter of courage? If not, what other things may have factored into the decision that led Jews to remain in Hitler's Europe?

Activities

- Mr. Wiesel says, "How I sympathized with Job!" With your group, study the Book of Job, found in the Tanach. Discuss why Wiesel compared his experiences to those of Job.

- In the very beginning of *Night,* Moshe the Beadle taught Eliezer that "Man questions God and God answers." Have your students make a list of questions they would like to ask God.

- Assign roles and read aloud "The Trial of God: A Play" by Elie Wiesel, Random House, 1995 (reprint edition).

No Pretty Pictures: A Child of War

By Anita Lobel
Greenwillow Books, 1998
208 pages
ISBN 0-688-15935-4
Grades 9-12

This National Book Award Finalist is a thoughtful, non-sentimental autobiography of two survivors of the Holocaust. Ms. Lobel briefly describes her family's life in Poland before the war, and focuses on how she and her brother managed to beat the odds and survive. They were hidden — they lived in a ghetto, in concentration camps, in prison, and in box cars, but somehow these two children lived to tell their story. After liberation, they were sent to Sweden and to a sanatorium. Eventually, they were reunited with their parents. The book is filled with reflections on doubt, suspicion, self-hatred, and shame. The author is able to describe what it was like from a child's perspective even as she looks back on it from adulthood.

Main Ideas

- Some children did survive the Holocaust, but lost their childhood.
- When people suffer physical hardship, things we take for granted are treasured.
- Reuniting with parents after the war was not always a joyful event.

Discussion Starters

- What does the author mean when she says, "Somewhere . . . my brother and I had been forced to leave ourselves"? What did the children do to survive?
- What did the Nazis rob from the author?
- At one point Ms. Lobel says, "I hoped she didn't expect the Jewish God to protect us." What do you think she meant by this?

Activities

 Have members of the group list the things they need to survive. Then have them list the things they need to be truly alive, happy, and safe. Place these things in an order of priority, and have the children indicate which things they have and which they don't have. Then, discuss which things they do not have that are truly important or necessary for a good life.

 In the course of the book, Anita Lobel turns her back on Judaism, and feels ashamed and angry about her Jewishness. Have the children write about an incident (real or imagined) in which their Jewishness made them uneasy, or one which made them feel glad to be Jewish.

 Anita Lobel has illustrated many books. Have your students visit libraries and bring in examples of her work. It is amazing that an early life filled with so much misery and hardship resulted in a woman capable of creating these joyful pictures.

For Further Reading

Grades K-3

Don't Forget by Patricia Lakin, illustrated by Ted Rand. Tambourine Books, 1994. 32 pages. ISBN 0-688-12076-8.

> In a very gently told story of a girl, Sarah, baking her very first cake, Ms. Lakin teaches the lesson that we should not forget. The Singers own the grocery store where Sarah has to buy some of the ingredients, but she hates going there because of the numbers on the Singers' arms. Without dwelling on them, mention is made of tattooed numbers, Europe, times gone by. Mrs. Singer teaches Sarah that the numbers should never be a secret. "If no one knows about bad things, they can happen all over again," she says. The book ends with Sarah's cake recipe.

Grades 3-5

Best Friends by Elizabeth Reuter (translated from the German). Pitspopany, 1993. 26 pages. ISBN 0-943706-18-1.

> In pre-war Germany, Judith and Lisa were best friends. Judith was Jewish, Lisa was not. But that didn't make any difference until Nazi doctrine began being taught in their school. They were told that good people had blonde hair and blue eyes. Lisa did. Bad people had hooked noses, dark hair, and a cunning look in their eyes. Judith had dark hair. At first, the girls were confused, but the more the lies were fed to them, the more they believed them. And then, a few days before *Kristallnacht,* the girls had a fight, different from the kind of fight that friends usually have. Judith did not return to school after that. And only after *Kristallnacht* did Judith realize she would never see her friend again.

Flowers on the Wall written and illustrated by Miriam Nerlove. Margaret K. McElderry Books, 1996. 32 pages. ISBN 0-689-50614-7.

> From one of the photographs of the late Roman Vishniac, the author has created a story describing the absolute poverty of a Jewish family in Warsaw in 1938. Rachel has no shoes and so cannot leave her one-windowed apartment during the long winter. Her father brings her some paints that a gentleman had given him, and together they start painting flowers on the walls. The book describes Rachel's family's hopes for the future, but the author makes it clear that those hopes were never realized. This picture book could be used in conjunction with *Children of a Vanished World* (edited by Mara Vishniac, translated by Miriam Hartman Flacks, University of California

Press, 1999), a book of Vishniac's work that captures Eastern European Jewish life before the war.

One Yellow Daffodil: A Hanukkah Story by David A. Adler, illustrated by Lloyd Bloom. Voyager Books, 1999. 32 pages. ISBN 0-15-202094-2.
    This is a very touching story of the loneliness that accompanies a Holocaust survivor. A florist, Morris Kaplan, leads a very quiet, isolated life. He befriends two school children who invite him to their home to celebrate Chanukah, a holiday he has not celebrated since he and his family were torn away from their home in Poland and from each other. This encounter opens a floodgate of memories and tears. The text is sparsely written and the accompanying pictures are dark.

A Picture Book of Anne Frank by David A. Adler, illustrated by Karen Ritz. Holiday House, 1993. 29 pages. ISBN 0-8234-1003-X.
    For children who are not yet old enough to read *Anne Frank: The Diary of a Young Girl*, this is a carefully written introduction to Anne Frank's life and diary. The vocabulary is suitable and the information straightforward, though harrowing.

Grades 4-6

After the War by Carol Matas. Aladdin Paperbacks, 1997. 133 pages. ISBN 0-68980-722-8.
    (See For Further Reading, Chapter 4, "History: 4,000 Years and Counting.")

Anne Frank: Life in Hiding by Johanna Hurwitz, illustrated by Vera Rosenberry. The Jewish Publication Society, 1989. 62 pages. ISBN 0-8276-0311-8.
    This is a matter-of-fact history of Anne Frank's story that is suitable for children not yet ready to tackle the emotions described in *Anne Frank: The Diary of a Young Girl*. It describes the historical context, the reason and details for hiding, or "diving" as the Dutch called it, and has an emphasis on the people who helped the Frank family and on the Dutch resistance. The book ends with a history of the diary itself.

Child of the Warsaw Ghetto by David A. Adler, illustrated by Karen Ritz. Holiday House, 1995. 32 pages. ISBN 0-8234-1160-5.
    In very plain language, Mr. Adler has provided a clear picture of the horrors of wartime Poland. This is a nonfiction account of Froim (later changed to Erwin) Baum, the youngest of seven children born to a poor Jewish couple in Warsaw. The book recounts his father's death, the family's destitute situation,

his life in a nurturing orphanage, and the rampages of the Holocaust. In a matter-of-fact way, the Ghetto is described, along with the living conditions, deaths, and "resettlement" actions. The inclusion of the Warsaw uprising and the survival of the main character make the book noteworthy.

Greater Than Angels by Carol Matas. Simon & Schuster Books for Young Readers, 1998. 133 pages. ISBN 0-689-81353-8.
  Told from the viewpoint of Anna, a teenaged German Jewish refugee, this book relates how she and many Jews and other refugees were protected and cared for by the pastors and villagers of the French town of Le Chambon-sur-Lignon during the Nazi occupation. This novel is based on true events which Matas seems to have researched quite extensively. It is rewarding to read about these simple people of good will who so courageously helped others for such a long period during those difficult times.

Hiding from the Nazis by David A. Adler, illustrated by Karen Ritz. Holiday House, 1997. 32 pages. ISBN 0-8234-1288-1.
  Like *Child of the Warsaw Ghetto* (see above), this book is a very straightforward, true account of a child who survived the Holocaust. In this instance, Lore Baer was successfully hidden with a Dutch farm family. Her parents survived as well, but when they came to retrieve Lore from the family who had protected her, the young girl was confused as to who her real family was. It took Lore many years to learn to trust and love her parents again.

Of Heroes, Hooks, and Heirlooms by Faye Silton. Jewish Publication Society, 1997. 99 pages. ISBN 0-8276-0649-4.
  This award winning short novel for young readers is a gentle introduction to the life of a Holocaust survivor's child and the special bonds and pressures that exist in her relationships with her parents. Mia, a young girl, wants to make her parents, especially her mother, happy again. In this search, she learns about family members who were killed in the Holocaust and about family traits and traditions that have endured.

Speed of Light by Sybil Rosen. Atheneum Books for Young Readers, 1999. 169 pages. ISBN 0-689-82437-8.
  The writing in this book is sometimes awkward and it is not Ms. Rosen at her best. Yet, the subject material and Audrey Ina, the 11-year-old protagonist, keep one's attention throughout this novel about the American South in the 1950s. Audrey Ina's *tante* (aunt) is a Holocaust survivor. She relives the horrors of her wartime experiences when Audrey Ina's father takes on the

status quo and helps an African-American in his quest for a position as a policeman. The backward Southern town reacts with anger, hatred, violence, and outright racism, much as in Nazi Germany. The aunt's most vivid flashbacks are of her brutal experiences in Auschwitz. The parallels to the position in which non-Jewish Germans found themselves are explored in a masterful fashion. There is a positive and hopeful resolution at the end of the book. This is a book best read with a parent.

Star of Fear, Star of Hope by Jo Hoestlandt, illustrated by Mark Polizzotti. Walker & Company, 2000 (reprint edition). 32 pages. ISBN 0-8027-7588-8.
This is a poignant story of the friendship between two girls in France during the Nazi occupation. One girl, Lydia, is Jewish. Her friend Helen is not. The story focuses on the night before Helen's birthday when Lydia has been given permission to stay overnight. A roundup of Jews began that night, and Lydia insisted on being taken home. Helen thought only of her birthday and her disappointment, and said something in anger she has always regretted. The two friends never saw each other again. This book leads beautifully into discussions about doing the right thing and about friendship.

The Upstairs Room by Johanna Reiss. Econo-Clad Books, 1999. 196 pages. ISBN 0-88103-981-0.
Based on Ms. Reiss's own wartime experiences, this is a moving account of the nearly three years that Annie and her sister Sini lived with the remarkable Oosterveld family in hiding. Her portrayal of herself, her family, and her rescuers is filled with interesting and realistic dialogue. The multitude of emotions shows the humanity of the characters and makes the era more understandable for this age group. This book was written almost 30 years ago. It is included here because it can contribute significantly to children's understanding of World War II. The sequel to this book is called *The Journey Back* by Johanna Reiss. Econo-Clad Books, 1999. (See For Further Reading, Chapter 4, "History: 4,000 Years and Counting.")

Grades 6-8
Daniel's Story by Carol Matas. Econo-Clad Books, 1999. Originally published in conjunction with the United States Holocaust Memorial Museum. 136 pages. ISBN 0-7857-1060-4.
Daniel is a fictitious character whose story is similar to that of many young Jewish men during the Holocaust. Written in the first person, this book describes the dangerous journeys Daniel and his family take from their home in Frankfurt to the Lodz ghetto in Poland, and then to the concentration

camps of Auschwitz and Buchenwald. Daniel survives the war and is able to find his girlfriend, Rosa, in what is left of the Lodz ghetto. Together, they plan a future in Palestine.

Dancing on the Bridge of Avignon by Ida Vos. Houghton Mifflin Company, 1995. 183 pages. ISBN 0-395-72039-7.
    The long list of "privileges" taken away from the Jews of Holland is a recurring theme in this book. The central figure of the story, ten-year-old Rosa, is a moody child. In her world, the adults try to protect the children right up to the point when they are rounded up for deportation. Rosa's story is based on the author's own experience during the war.

Rose Blanche written and illustrated by Roberto Innocenti. Econo-Clad Books, 1999. 32 pages. ISBN 0-613-13007-3.
    Illustrated with somewhat surreal pictures, this book tells a story of a young German girl who follows her best instincts and feeds starving concentration camp inmates. The narrative makes it clear that Rose Blanche has no idea about what is really happening in and around her in her small German town. Just before liberation, Rose Blanche is killed in the confusion.

Ten Thousand Children by Anne L. Fox and Eva Abraham-Podietz. Behrman House, Inc., 1998. 128 pages. ISBN 0-87441-648-5.
    This book is subtitled *True Stories Told by Children Who Escaped the Holocaust on the Kindertransport*. It is put together like a scrapbook with photographs, different kinds of lettering, and graphics. The chapters cover life under Hitler, the journey to safety, and life after the war. Each of the children featured in the book describes life during the war, and the reader is told what has happened to them since. Words and phrases are defined in margin notes.

Grades 9-12

Elie Wiesel: A Voice for Humanity by Ellen Norman Stern. Jewish Publication Society, 1996. 168 pages. ISBN 0-8276-0574-9.
    This is a clearly written biography of the Nobel Peace Prize winner. It describes his complex life in pre-war Hungary, the horrors of his experiences at the hands of the Nazis, and his life since, during which he has grappled with the meaning of those experiences.

Four Perfect Pebbles: A Holocaust Story by Lila Perl and Marion Blumenthal Lazan. Greenwillow Books, 1996. 132 pages. ISBN 0-688-14294-X.
    Marion Blumenthal Lazan survived refugee, transit, and prison camps, and — after the war — displaced person camps. She describes her HIAS

sponsorship in the United States and her eventual resumption of a "normal" life. This is a straightforward, sometimes graphic account of her lost childhood at the hands of the Nazis.

Rescue: The Story of How Gentiles Saved Jews in the Holocaust by Milton Meltzer. Harper & Row, Publishers, 1988. 168 pages. ISBN 0-06-024210-8.
Using eyewitness accounts, along with diaries, letters, and memoirs, the author has compiled dozens of stories about courageous deeds performed in the face of brutal racism. The book is a call to remember the moral choices and actions made by some during a time when so many stood by silently.

Teen Witnesses to the Holocaust. A series edited by Yaffa Eliach.
These nine powerful books are printed on glossy paper with black and white photographs. The information is very accessible to teens and is designed to help them imagine themselves in the situations Jewish teens in Europe faced in the 1930s and 40s.

The Hidden Children of the Holocaust: Teens Who Hid from the Nazis by Esther Kustanowitz. The Rosen Publishing Group, Inc., 1999. 64 pages. ISBN 0-8239-2562-5.

Rescuers Defying the Nazis: Non-Jewish Teens Who Rescued Jews by Toby Axelrod. The Rosen Publishing Group, Inc., 1999. 64 pages. ISBN 0-8239-2848-9.

In the Ghettos: Teens Who Survived the Ghettos of the Holocaust by Eleanor H. Ayer. The Rosen Publishing Group, Inc., 1999. 64 pages. ISBN 0-8239-2845-4.

Liberation: Teens in the Concentration Camps and the Teen Soldiers Who Liberated Them by Tina E. Tito. The Rosen Publishing Group, Inc., 1998. 64 pages. ISBN 0-8239-2846-2.

Escape: Teens Who Escaped the Holocaust To Freedom by Sandra Giddens. The Rosen Publishing Group, Inc., 1998. 64 pages. ISBN 0-8239-2843-8.

The Hitler Youth: Marching toward Madness by Alexa Dvorson. The Rosen Publishing Group, Inc., 1998. 64 pages. ISBN 0-8239-2783-0.

Resistance: Teen Partisans and Resisters Who Fought Nazi Tyranny by Alexa Dvorson. The Rosen Publishing Group, Inc., 1998. 64 pages. ISBN 0-8239-2847-0.

In the Camps: Teens Who Survived the Nazi Concentration Camps by Toby Axelrod. The Rosen Publishing Group, Inc., 1999. 64 pages. ISBN 0-8239-2844-6.

In My Hands: Memories of a Holocaust Rescuer by Irene Gut Opdyke with Jennifer Armstrong. Alfred A. Knopf, Inc., 1999. 280 pages. ISBN 0-679-89181-1.
   (See Featured Books, Chapter 2, "Ethics: Doing the Right Thing.")

Chapter 7

Life Cycle: To Everything There Is a Season

Birth, Bar and Bat Mitzvah, marriage, divorce, illness, aging, and death are just some of the topics touched on in this chapter. Judaism provides a framework for negotiating both joyous and sad occasions. For example, when Sue's daughter and her son were born, wonderful rituals marked their welcome into the Jewish community and into the family's community. Those rituals — a baby naming and a *Brit Milah* — made happy and exciting times even more joyous. The ceremonies also gave close family and friends roles to play as godparents, as members of a *minyan* reciting prayers, and as the *sandek*, who holds the baby during the ceremony. There may soon be other meaningful occasions for her family — a Bat Mitzvah and a Bar Mitzvah, Confirmation, and eventually weddings. The books in this chapter help children to understand these important life cycle events through fiction and non-fiction.

Featured Books

Pearl's Marigolds for Grandpa (PK)
The Biggest Littlest Birthday Cake (K-3)
The Keeping Quilt (K-3)
Sophie's Name (K-3)
Gabriel's Ark (2-4)
Grandpa's Gamble (2-4)
Remember That (2-4)
Terrible, Terrible! (2-4)
Pink Slippers, Bat Mitzvah Blues (4-6)
For Kids — Putting God on Your Guest List (6-8)
When Bad Things Happen To Good People (9-12)

Pearl's Marigolds for Grandpa

Written and illustrated by Jane Breskin Zalben
Simon & Schuster Books For Young Readers, 1997
22 pages
ISBN 0-689-80448-2
PK

When Pearl's Grandpa dies, she wonders who will read stories to her, play checkers with her, and send her marigold seeds in the spring. She struggles through the initial mourning period (during which many Jewish customs are explained). Eventually, she comes to realize that Grandpa's memory is alive within her, and that some of their shared experiences — such as the planting of marigolds — can continue. Such sensitive issues are handled simply and reassuringly. Ms. Zalben also discusses the funeral rituals of many of the world's major religions.

Main Ideas

- There comes a time when people die.
- We are usually very sad when someone we love dies.
- Our memories of people who have died can keep them alive within us.

Discussion Starters

- Have you known someone who has died? Who were they? How did you feel when they died? To whom did you speak about your feelings?
- Have you ever been to a funeral? What happens at a funeral?
- What is something you could say to a friend who lost someone close to them?

Activities

 Invite children who have suffered losses to talk about special things they used to do with loved ones who have died. Then, as Pearl did with her father, see if there is someone else with whom they can maintain that activity.

 Talk about a famous Jewish person who recently died and was written up in the newspaper. Read the obituary to the children. Then write a condolence card to the person's family.

 Buy giant orange marigold seeds and plant them with your class. Put them by a window. Make a poster which shows that these plants are "Pearl's Marigolds for Grandpa." Have all the children participate in planting and then caring for them. Perhaps each child can give a plant in bloom as a special gift to someone they love.

The Biggest Littlest Birthday Cake

By Yaffa Ganz
Illustrated by Harvey Klineman
Feldheim Publishers, 1992
30 pages
ISBN 0-87306-602-2
K-3

A verse in *Pirke Avot* ends with the words: "Go out and see what is the proper way to behave . . . be generous and look upon everyone with a 'good eye' . . . find a good friend . . . have a good heart." This story shows the wisdom of this advice. In this tale of their mutual birthday and their desire to make each other happy, Mimmy and Simmy learn what friendship and sharing are all about. It is also important to see how when the girls get stuck, their parents get involved and help them overcome their difficulty.

Main Ideas

- Friendships are important.
- Choosing a birthday present takes careful thought.
- Problems in a friendship can be worked out.

Discussion Starters

- What was your favorite thing that Mimmy did? that Simmy did?
- Do you think the mothers were right to get involved in their daughters' problem? Why or why not?
- How did you like the ending? Was it realistic — was it something that could actually have happened?

Activities

 Have children list what they like about birthdays. Review the list with the class.

 Pick two students whose birthdays are close together and have them bring in a treat for each other. Discuss whether or not this was a success, and why.

 Have the class bake a cake together. At a birthday party for the whole class, share the cake and sing "Happy Birthday" to everyone.

The Keeping Quilt

Written and illustrated by Patricia Polacco
Simon and Schuster Books for Young Readers,
1998 (revised edition)
32 pages
ISBN 0-689-82090-9
Grades K-3

Every so often, we read a great book. This is one of them. This Jewish immigrant story is so warm and loving that it brings tears to the eyes. Through her pictures and her words, Patricia Polacco engages adults and children alike as she tells the story of her family and the quilt that comforted them and which they used through the generations.

Main Ideas

- People moved to America from European countries.
- Meaningful objects have been handed down through various generations.
- In some communities, Judaism has changed over the years.

Discussion Starter

- Patricia Polacco drew only the cloth of the quilt in color. Did you find that to be odd? interesting? Explain your answers.
- What item does your family have that has been handed down through the generations?
- Have you ever seen a real quilt? Where? Describe it.

Activities

- Make a class quilt. Have each child bring in an old item of clothing and make a square out of it. Have the children do as much of the project themselves as is possible. Display the finished product in the classroom or the hallway.

- See if your class can attend a wedding ceremony at a local synagogue. Ask for impressions. Afterward, explain and discuss the various aspects of the ceremony. (If you can't arrange attendance at a real wedding, stage a mock wedding.)

- Make up packages for the next few upcoming weddings at a local synagogue. Include all the components listed in the book.

Sophie's Name

By Phyllis Grodes
Illustrated by Shelly O. Haas
Kar-Ben Copies, Inc., 1990
32 pages
ISBN 0-929371-18-6
K-3

Sophie Davida Finkle-Cohen, who is seven and a half, decides her name is too long and changes it to Sue Ann. Her family goes along with her, but through stories about each of her names, they lovingly tell her why she was given each of the four names. Passover, immigration to America, and her family history are explored through these stories. At the end of the book, realizing how unique her name is, Sophie says, "Twenty-three letters, two spaces, and one dash. A name from Poland and a name from the Bible. And one name made out of two."

Main Ideas

- Your name was probably given to you for an important reason.
- Names can help to keep alive the memories of our deceased relatives.
- Sometimes we can learn to like things when we understand why they are what they are.

Discussion Starters

- How many people here like their name? How many don't? If you could, to what would you change your name?
- Do you know why you were given the name you have?
- Do you think that people would treat you differently if you had a different name?

Activities

 Have the children find out why they were given each of their names (first, middle, and last). Then have each child share the "story" of their names with the rest of the class.

 Have each child pick names they would like to give to their children. Have each explain why he/she chose those names.

 Give each child a large piece of paper and on it write his/her name vertically. Then have each make an acrostic using the letters of their name to begin different words that describe them. Children can also decorate the paper with pictures that portray themselves. Each can then share the acrostic with the class.

    Example: **S**pecial
                         Unusual
                         Excellent

Gabriel's Ark

Sandra R. Curtis
Alef Design, 1999
64 pages
ISBN 1-881283-22-4
Grades 2-4

This fictional account movingly describes what it might be like to have a brother with very special needs. The narrator of the story is Gabriel's younger sister, Leah. She describes a loving home with all the resources it would take to provide an ideal situation for a child as severely handicapped as Gabriel. The nature of his condition is never named in the book, but he is small, weak, and mentally disabled. As his thirteenth birthday approaches, Gabriel's family, along with their Rabbi, provide a framework in which this special child can become a Bar Mitzvah in synagogue before his family and community.

Main Ideas

- Some people are born with special needs.

- Each person is expected to do the best they can with the abilities with which they are born.

- Families can work together to make difficult situations better.

Discussion Starters

- Do you know anyone with special needs? In what way is that person different from you? In what way is that person the same as you?

- Why do you think it was important for Gabriel's family to find a way for him to have a Bar Mitzvah ceremony?

- Gabriel's favorite Bible story is Noah's Ark. Why do you think it is his favorite? What is your favorite Bible story? Why is it special for you?

Activities

After the flood, God promises Noah and his family that there will never again be a flood to destroy the earth (Genesis 9:11). When children become B'nai Mitzvah, they are making a promise to follow the commandments, the *mitzvot*. In study pairs, have students brainstorm promises they can make (1) to themselves, (2) to one another, (3) to their teachers, and (4) to their families. Then, have each group decide on the most important promise in each of those four categories. Join together and have each pair report their decisions and explain why they made the choices they did. To remind the students of their promises, record the promises on a chart in the classroom. (If desired, the children can decorate the chart with rainbows.)

Gabriel's task at his Bar Mitzvah service is to recite the *"Shema"* with his sisters. When the time comes, he refuses, but then, all by himself he says: "Hear, Israel. One God. Rainbow promise." Study the *"Shema"* with your students, then have them rewrite it in their own words. Have a brief worship service in the classroom and substitute the prayers the children wrote for the *"Shema."*

Invite someone who works with special needs children to visit your class and explain what individuals can do to help children with disabilities.

Grandpa's Gamble

By Richard Michelson
Illustrated by Barry Moser
Marshall Cavendish Corporation, 1999
32 pages
ISBN 0-7614-5034-3
Grades 2-4

This beautifully written book deals with the life choices we have to make and with the difficulties that life often presents. Two young children learn about their grandfather as a young man, his immigration to America, how he gambled to survive, the love he had for their grandmother, and the changes he made in his life as part of a deal with God. The illustrations — executed in graphite with sepia washes, heightened with chalk and Chinese White — are extremely unusual.

Main Ideas

- The early life of older people can often be very interesting.

- Love is the most powerful motivator of all.

- Many of the Jews who immigrated to the United States early in the 1900s had a very difficult time surviving.

Discussion Starters

- What did you think of Grandpa Sam's gambling? Do you feel he had a choice? Explain your answer.

- When Grandpa Sam said his "parents had not sent me to a new land to learn to cheat and steal," did you agree? What were the reasons his parents had sent him to America?

- Grandpa Sam's parents told him that "It is children . . . that make a man wealthy." What does that mean? Do you agree, or do you think there are other things that make a person wealthy? Explain your answer.

Activities

 Have the children use a deck of cards in a way that is different from what they were designed for (e.g., make a card collage, a house of cards, or use them to decorate good cheer or holiday cards to be sent to shut-ins or elderly residents of a nursing home).

Have each student ask his/her grandparents (or another older person) to think of something they did when they were a child, adolescent, or young adult that would surprise those who know them now. Ask each child to write, tape, or video their story and share it with the class. (Be sure the grandparent/older person agrees.)

This story of a poor immigrant is very poignant. Suggest ways your class can help recent immigrants to America. They might have a car wash or bake sale to raise money, then donate it to HIAS, to a local Jewish Family Service, or to another worthwhile organization that helps immigrants.

Remember That

By Lesléa Newman
Illustrated by Karen Ritz
Clarion Books, 1996
32 pages
ISBN 0-395-66156-0
Grades 2-4

This moving book tells of a little girl and her Bubbe who always celebrate Shabbos together. When the story begins, Bubbe lives in her own apartment. She makes delicious soup every week which she and the girl enjoy together. Bubbe grows older and moves in with the girl and her mother, who takes over making the soup (which is okay, but not as good as Bubbe's). Although the girl is sad about these developments, she is happy about seeing Bubbe every day and being able to spend time with her. As Bubbe and the girl age, Bubbe becomes so enfeebled that she must go to live in a nursing home. The girl visits her, joins her in eating chicken soup (which is very bad). While she is sad, the girl realizes that they still can visit and have Shabbos together. Most important, she realizes their love remains unchanged. Bubbe's positive and hopeful attitude throughout the book softens these difficult issues.

Main Ideas

- People grow older, and physically cannot always do what they could before.
- Special relationships can endure through many difficulties.
- Shabbos is a special time for family to come together.

Discussion Starters

- How old is your oldest living relative? Where does he/she live? How often do you see him/her?
- What do you think is the best thing about getting older?

Do you think that Bubbe gives the little girl good advice in the book? Why or why not?

Activities

 Teach your class to play *Knock Rummy* and *Crazy Eights*. Let them play for a while, just as the little girl and her Bubbe did.

 Have your class draw or paint some pictures that they can bring to a local nursing home to brighten up the residents' rooms or a common area.

 Have your class make chicken soup with *matzah* balls (if time is an issue, use the packaged soup and *matzah* ball mix). Have each child invite one special person to join the class in eating the soup.

Terrible, Terrible! A Folktale Retold

By Robin Bernstein
Illustrated by Shauna Mooney Kawasaki
Kar-Ben Copies, Inc., 1998
32 pages
ISBN 1-58013-016-X
Grades 2-4

This is a wonderful, bright, funny book that deals with the issues of remarriage, blended families, and the wisdom of Rabbis. When Abigail's mother gets married to a man with four children and they all move in together, Abigail is overwhelmed by the clutter and chaos. Her mother and stepfather agree to try any idea she might have, so off she goes to her Rabbi (who just happens to be an attractive, professional looking woman). The Rabbi suggests first bringing in the bicycles, then the pets, then their cousins, and finally tells them to take everything out. The house, of course, seems much bigger than before, and everyone is now satisfied with the space they have.

Main Ideas

- It can be difficult to have two families come together and live as one.
- Solutions are not always immediately obvious.
- Rabbis can be very helpful solving problems of everyday life.

Discussion Starters

- What was your favorite scene in the book, and why?
- What did you think of the Rabbi's first suggestion? her second? her third? her last?
- Do you know anyone who is a member of a blended family?

Activities

 Ask one of the children from your class to share their experiences as a member of a blended family (or invite an older student to come in and speak). Ask the presenter to think of some funny stories about learning to live together.

 Challenge your class to come up with other suggestions, different from the Rabbi's, of things to bring into the house. Have them list their reasons for their choices.

 Find a version of the original folktale and read it with your class. (See *It Could Always Be Worse*, Chapter 3, "Folklore: From Generation To Generation.") Compare and contrast this version to *Terrible, Terrible!* Discuss which version the students like better, and why. Ask: Did Ms. Bernstein do a good job of updating this folktale and making it relevant to modern day life?

Pink Slippers, Bat Mitzvah Blues

By Ferida Wolff
The Jewish Publication Society, 1995
(reissue edition)
137 pages
ISBN 0-8276-0531-5
Grades 4-6

After her Bat Mitzvah, all Alyssa wanted to do was practice at the dance studio. Other people intruded on her dancing dreams — her Rabbi would not stop pressuring her to join the Confirmation class, and then her best friend got very sick and needed her to visit. Ms. Wolff explores in a thoughtful manner the central conflict in this book — how Alyssa dealt with these demands while trying to juggle a role in "The Nutcracker." This novel explores the turmoil experienced by many young teenagers who are learning to understand their Jewish identity and their place in the world, particularly in the post Bar or Bat Mitzvah years.

Main Ideas

 People often have to make choices between many important things in their lives.

 Figuring out what is most important at any one moment can be very difficult.

 Being Jewish is not just about studying for a Bar or Bat Mitzvah ceremony.

Discussion Starters

- Have you ever had to make the kind of difficult decision that Alyssa did when she chose visiting Ellen over her role in "The Nutcracker"?

- What do you hope to learn by continuing your Jewish education after you become a Bar or Bat Mitzvah?

- Do you think Alyssa did the "right thing" when she sneaked into the hospital to visit Ellen, breaking the hospital rules, but performing the *mitzvah* of visiting the ill?

Activities

 Make an overall list of all of the activities in which your students are involved, other than public/private school and Hebrew school. Don't forget to include those that are not organized (visiting the elderly or sick, doing *tzedakah*). Discuss with your students the relative importance of these activities. Have them make an individual list and rank the items in descending order of importance. When they are finished, have them share their lists and discuss what is really important.

 The idea of a worship service run by and choreographed by the students is a wonderful one. Arrange with your synagogue an opportunity for students so they can add their personal talents (poetry, dance, etc.) to a service.

 Rabbi Pearlman is a warm and sympathetic character who exemplifies the best of being a Rabbi and being Jewish. He is supportive, caring, and informative. Is there anyone like this in your school or synagogue? If so, and your students agree, think of something that they can do for that person (such as the Jarred Judaism that Alyssa made for Rabbi Pearlman) as a way of thanking them for their efforts and their achievements.

For Kids — Putting God on Your Guest List

By Rabbi Jeffrey K. Salkin
Jewish Lights Publishing, 1998
134 pages
ISBN 1-58023-015-6
Grades 6-8

Putting God on the Guest List is an award winning Bar/Bat Mitzvah handbook for parents about reclaiming the spiritual meaning of this life cycle event. This is the kids' companion to that book. Here Rabbi Salkin explains the core values of Judaism and of the Bar/Bat Mitzvah process. He discusses in depth what it means to be a Jew, why kids should choose to be a part of Judaism, and how Judaism can play a part in their lives after "the big event." There is a glossary of frequently used Hebrew words and a section with suggestions for *tzedakah* and the performance of other *mitzvot*.

Main Ideas

- Becoming a Bar/Bat Mitzvah is something which requires a great deal of thought.

- There is much more to becoming a Bar/Bat Mitzvah than a party.

- There is a variety of different ways to make your Bar/Bat Mitzvah celebration meaningful.

Discussion Starters

- Do you think there is a need for a book like Rabbi Salkin's?

- Which part of the book was the most interesting? Was there a topic you didn't know about before reading this book?

- Are you planning on doing anything differently for your Bar/Bat Mitzvah as a result of reading this book?

Activities

 At the end of each of the nine chapters, Rabbi Salkin has a section of questions designed to engage his readers and to give them an opportunity to think about and respond to what they have just read. In addition to reading the book, assign these questions as homework. Check to make sure they were taken seriously. (There are no right or wrong answers to these questions.)

 As a follow-up to the third question above, help students come up with something special they want to do at their Bar/Bat Mitzvah. If they are having difficulty thinking of something, suggest they find a charity from the list at the end of the book and donate some money to it in honor of the event.

 Send home a letter asking the parents to read this book or the adult version, *Putting God on the Guest List*. Then, in a group that includes both the students and their parents, facilitate a discussion to assist the families in creating a meaningful family event.

When Bad Things Happen To Good People

By Harold S. Kushner
Schocken Books, 1981
(2nd edition preface, 1989)
148 pages
ISBN 0-8052-4089-6
Grades 9-12

Terrible things can happen to people. Some things can be so bad that they shake one's faith in God. Rabbi Harold Kushner wrote this book in response to the death of his 14-year-old son and as a way of examining this tragedy in the context of his belief in God. This lucid and profound discourse provides insight and reassurance. It also deals head-on with those issues we cannot avoid (death, illness, etc.). Facing life's trials and coming to some sort of terms with them are two of the most important life skills a person needs to acquire to be whole and to be able to enjoy those aspects of life that are wonderful. Although this book was written 20 years ago, its lessons are timeless.

Main Ideas

 Bad things can happen to anyone, and there is nothing we can do to prevent this.

 God does not help us avoid our tragedies, but can help us in dealing with them.

 Many well-known stories from the Jewish tradition can be viewed from a different perspective, one in which God is not ultimately responsible.

Discussion Starters

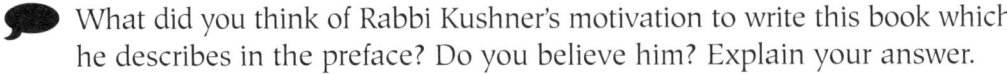 What did you think of Rabbi Kushner's motivation to write this book which he describes in the preface? Do you believe him? Explain your answer.

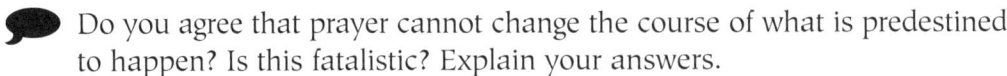 Do you agree that prayer cannot change the course of what is predestined to happen? Is this fatalistic? Explain your answers.

💬 Have you ever prayed during a difficult time and then found/been given the strength to go on?

Activities

🤝 Help your class reach out to someone who feels alone with their troubles. Have students come up with an appropriate way of showing their support. Perhaps they could cook and deliver a meal to the person in need.

📄 Have each student write an essay about the worst tragedy that has happened to them. If (and only if) they feel comfortable doing so, have them share what they have written in pairs or with the class as a whole.

🗣 Have a therapist come in to discuss the various stages of dealing with grief or loss. This will enable students to have an opportunity for questions and discussions.

For Further Reading

PK

Beni's First Wedding story and pictures by Jane Breskin Zalben. Henry Holt and Company. 1998. 32 pages. ISBN 0-8050-4846-4.

This is an appealing introduction to the Jewish wedding, and it includes many of the religious aspects of that life cycle event. There is also an explanation of the customs of other religions, as well as a recipe for Mama's Honey Wedding Cake.

Pushkin Meets the Bundle by Harriet M. Ziefert, illustrated by Donald Saaf. Atheneum Books for Young Readers, 1998. 32 pages. ISBN 0-689-81413-5.

In this fabulously beautiful book, Harriet Ziefert humorously and gently looks at what bringing home a new baby does to the youngster that is already in residence. This is an excellent book to use with young children expecting their first, or even subsequent, sibling.

Grades K-3

Baby's Bris by Susan Wilkowski, illustrated by Judith Friedman. Kar-Ben Copies, Inc., 1999. 32 pages. ISBN 1-58013-052-6.

During the first eight days of her brother's life, Sophie is introduced to the joy and ceremonies that accompany the birth of a Jewish male. Her family treats her with great sensitivity so that she, too, feels special and proud. After the *bris* (circumcision ceremony), Sophie holds her baby brother and says, "You try to be good." This is her first contribution to her brother's Jewish education. The *Brit Milah* itself is handled very sensitively and inoffensively. In end notes, there is an explanation of the *mitzvah* of circumcision and a glossary.

Grandma's Soup by Nancy Karkowsky, illustrated by Shelly O. Haas. Kar-Ben Copies, Inc., 1989. 32 pages. ISBN 0-930494-97-7.

This is a very touching and sensitive discussion of the difficulties that Alzheimer's Disease can cause in families and how it can affect relationships. It is told from the point of view of Eve, a little girl whose grandmother has this disease. It explores the impact of her grandmother's forgetfulness (such as how to make the Shabbat soup or who Eve is) on all of the relatives, as well as their valiant attempts to maintain loving ties despite the limitations imposed by the disease.

Grades 2-4

For Heaven's Sake by Sandy Eisenberg Sasso, illustrated by Kathryn Kunz Finney. Jewish Lights Publishing, 1999. 32 pages. ISBN 1-58023-054-7.

When Isaiah's grandfather died, Isaiah's mother told him that Grandpa went to heaven to be with God. Now, several months later, Isaiah is determined to find out exactly what and where heaven is. He asks different people in his life, but does not get a satisfactory answer until his widowed grandmother tries to explain. She takes him to several places where Grandpa had spent time — the soup kitchen, the library, and choir rehearsal. At the end of a delightful day, Isaiah's grandmother explains, "Heaven is often in places we are least likely to look . . . I feel there is a part of Grandpa in all the places and people we visited today, and a little of heaven, too." Rabbi Sasso has successfully tackled an abstract idea, presenting it in a way that young children can understand.

My Brother's Bar Mitzvah written by Janet Gallant, illustrated by Susan Avishai. Kar-Ben Copies, Inc., 1990. 32 pages. ISBN 0-929371-20-8.

When nine-year-old Sarah's older brother is busy preparing for his upcoming Bar Mitzvah, everyone keeps saying that he will "become a man." This is hard for her to understand, despite being around for all of the preparations. But she begins to figure it out on the day of the actual Bar Mitzvah when she sees how grown-up her brother acts. This is an excellent introduction to what a Bar Mitzvah is, and the preparations involved in planning for one, from the perspective of the parents, siblings, and honoree.

Grades 3-5

About the B'nai Bagels by E.L. Konigsburg. Yearling Books, 1985 (reissue edition). 172 pages. ISBN 0-440-40034-1.

When Mark Setzer, who is 12 years old, lost his best friend and had to begin really studying hard for his upcoming Bar Mitzvah, he thought he had enough to deal with. Little did he realize things could get worse — his mother becomes his Little League manager and makes his older brother the team coach! This classic young adult novel deals with familial issues, religious responsibilities, making choices, and growing up. An excellent recommendation for a pre-Bar/Bat Mitzvah reader.

The Always Prayer Shawl by Sheldon Oberman, illustrated by Ted Lewin. Boyds Mill Press, 1994. 36 pages. ISBN 1-878093-22-3.

In this moving book about handing down religious tradition through the generations, we follow Adam as he leaves Czarist Russia, emigrates to

America, grows up, and grows old. He holds onto the prayer shawl his grandfather gave him when he left Russia, using it every week, repairing it, and telling his grandson that one day it will be his. He also tells his grandson what his own grandfather taught him: " . . . some things change and some things don't." This truism, and the reality of time passing, are central themes in the book, and can be used in teaching aging, continuity, and tradition.

Strudel Stories by Joanne Rocklin. Delacorte Press, 1999. 131 pages. ISBN 0-385-32602-5.
When discussing death, this book may be helpful. (See Featured Books, Chapter 4, "History: 4,000 Years and Counting.")

Grades 4-6

Are You There, God? It's Me, Margaret by Judy Blume. Laurel Leaf, 1991. 149 pages. ISBN 0-440-90419-6.
Judy Blume wrote this book over 30 years ago, yet many of the topics she deals with are still important and relevant. Margaret Simon is 11, going on 12. This book chronicles her move from New York City to New Jersey and her first year in the suburbs. As the child of a Jewish father and a Christian mother, both of whom turned their backs on religion, Margaret feels connected to God, but not religion. The issues of religious belief, her search for God in religion, becoming an adolescent, and fitting in with new friends and family are just some of the topics explored in this book.

Dear Elijah: A Passover Story by Miriam Bat-Ami. The Jewish Publication Society, 1995. 106 pages. ISBN 0-8276-0592-7.
This is an interesting introduction to Elijah as told through the "diary" that 11-year-old Rebecca Samuelson keeps around Passover time when her father is ill. Religious observance, one's place or role in their family, loss, holiday celebrations, and introspection are just some of the weighty issues touched on by this book.

Lost and Found: A Kid's Book for Living through Loss by Marc Gellman and Thomas Hartman. Illustrated by Debbie Tilley. New York: Morrow Junior Books a division of William Morrow and Company, Inc., 1999. 176 pages. ISBN 0-688-15752-1.
The authors draw on years of counseling experience to suggest universal truths to help people of any religion live and grow through losses large and small. The book is simply written and uses humor when appropriate. Younger children will need an adult to read relevant chapters to them. Older children

can read the book on their own, but discussion with an adult about the nature of a particular loss is very much in order.

Grades 4-8
Bar Mitzvah: A Jewish Boy's Coming of Age by Eric A. Kimmel, illustrated by Erika Weihs. Penguin, 1997. 143 pages. ISBN 0-614-28899-1.

This is a good book for a boy to read prior to his Bar Mitzvah, or for anyone who wants to learn about what a Bar Mitzvah represents in Judaism. This life cycle event is put into religious and historical perspective in this book. In addition, there is an excellent overview of Judaism and synagogue services. Anecdotal stories interspersed between the chapters pertain to several men's experiences surrounding their Bar Mitzvah.

Grades 6-8
Bar Mitzvah Lessons by Martin Elsant. Alef Design Group, 1993. 96 pages. ISBN 0-881283-01-1.

David's fear of performing in front of people at his upcoming Bar Mitzvah causes him to alienate five different tutors as a way of avoiding the whole event. His father demonstrates his love for him and willingness to try anything to help David by hiring an eccentric former Yeshiva teacher-turned-mechanic named Reuven Weiss. Their journey through David's portion of the Torah, and the relationship that develops between them as they study together, enable David to learn a great deal about Judaism, growing up, facing one's fears, and the meaning of bravery.

Grades 6 and up
With All My Heart, With All My Mind: Thirteen Stories about Growing Up Jewish edited by Sandy Asher. Simon & Schuster Books For Young Readers, 1999. 164 pages. ISBN 0-689-82012-7.

In this wonderfully written anthology, 13 of the leading Jewish authors of our day have contributed stories and post-story discussions about growing up Jewish and what that meant to them. There are many different experiences and genres presented in these short stories, and each makes a unique point and contribution to the ongoing dialogue between Jews and their religion/culture/heritage/you name it. This book would be an excellent Bar or Bat Mitzvah present for the serious teenage reader.

How Good Do We Have to Be? A New Understanding of Guilt and Forgiveness by Harold S. Kushner. Little, Brown, and Company, 1996. 181 pages. ISBN 0-316-51933-2.

This is an ideal book for those suffering from existential and/or adolescent angst. In this short book, Rabbi Kushner continues the living message of religion and of God found in his book *When Bad Things Happen To Good People*. Here the message is broadened through a discussion of the myth of perfection in our lives and how this myth leads to unnecessary misery and unhappiness. Rabbi Kushner presents a unique and radical interpretation of the story of Adam and Eve, asserting that eating from the Tree of Knowledge was a positive act which gave humankind true humanity. Work, sexuality and childbearing, and a sense of our own mortality, the three "punishments" that resulted from that act are actually positive contributions to our living meaningful and worthwhile lives.

Grades 9-12

Growing Up Jewish: An Anthology edited by Bill Adler, introduction by Jay David. Diane Publishing Co., 1997. 223 pages. ISBN 0-7781-6704-9.

This outstanding anthology brings together 25 selections by American Jewish authors, some short stories, and some excerpts from novels or autobiographies. The book is divided into three sections: Part I – "Making Our Way," which is devoted to stories of first generation immigrants to the United States and the obstacles that they faced; Part II – "Discovering Americanness," which explores how the children of the original immigrants bridged the gap between the old world of their parents and their new one; and, Part III – "New Voices," which is a selection of new writings about growing up Jewish in America. These stories of childhood and adolescence explore issues of Jewish identity, language, generational differences, family life, many rites of passage, and the difficulties of coming of age.

To Begin Again: The Journey toward Comfort, Strength and Faith in Difficult Times by Naomi Levy. Ballantine Publishing Group, 1999. 267 pages. ISBN 0-345-41383-0.

In this interesting book, Rabbi Levy explores both the stages of grief she felt after her father's murder, when she was 15, and the many painful experiences of her congregants in Venice, California. She speaks knowledgeably about the process of mourning and rebuilding a life after a loss or trauma. Her story is woven with the stories of others, along with the wisdom of Judaism and its great sages. Interspersed are beautiful, original, nondenominational prayers which she wrote that serve as reminders of the good in life and the strength we can all find within ourselves. This book can be a powerful tool in learning those things over which we have control and those over which we don't, what we can do about our sorrows and what we can't, and the role that God can play in our lives.

All Ages

To Every Thing There Is a Season: Verses from Ecclesiastes illustrations and afterword by Leo and Diane Dillon. Scholastic, Inc., 1998. 30 pages. ISBN 0-590-47887-7.

The poet Alfred Lord Tennyson is quoted in the preface to this stunning book, calling Ecclesiastes "the greatest poem of ancient or modern times." Leo and Diane Dillon have paired the timeless verses from the Book of Ecclesiastes with illustrations inspired by diverse art from different historical eras and from around the world. The endnotes include information about these different art forms. This book could be used to initiate a conversation about the inevitabilities of life. Note: The authors have used the King James Version of the Bible for their translation.